Walter L. Wilmshurst

Hand-Drawn Portrait by Jessica Naomi

Walter L. Wilmshurst

Hand-Drawn Portrait by Jessica Naomi

Walter L. Wilmshurst
Forgotten Essays

Darrell Jordan

Athenaia.Co

Walter L. Wilmshurst Forgotten Essays - Compiled with graphics and edits by Darrell Jordan, Copyright © First Edition 2024. All rights reserved.

No part of this book may be reproduced in
whole or in part without the written
permission from the publisher, nor stored in any retrieval
system or transmitted by
any means, electronic, mechanical, photocopying,
recording, or other, without the
written consent of the publisher.
For bulk purchases, please contact the publisher.
Enquiry@Athenaia.Co
Library of Congress Cataloging-in Publication Data
Names: Wilmshurst, Walter | Jordan, Darrell
Title: Walter L. Wilmshurst Forgotten Essays - Darrell Jordan, MPS
Description: First U.S. edition. | Coeur D'Alene, Idaho: Athenaia [2024]
Identifiers: LCCN (pending) |
ISBN 979-8-88556-052-8 (First Edition hardcover)
Subjects: OCC016000: BODY, MIND & SPIRIT / Occultism |
HI036000: PHILOSOPHY / Hermeneutics |
REL047000: RELIGION / Mysticism
LC record available at https://lccn. loc.gov

On the internet: Parallel47North.com/collections/esoteric-books
Managing Editor: Darrell Jordan
Original Author and Essay: Walter L. Wilmshurst
Executive Producer: Yuka Jordan
Book Cover Design by Yuka Jordan
Book Cover Art and Illustrations: Jessica Naomi
Image Credits: Walter L. Wilmshurst's and Darrell Jordan's personal collection
Printed and bound in the United States

Publisher: Athenaia, LLC
2370 N Merritt Crk Lp, Ste 1
Coeur D'Alene, ID 83814
The United States

Let me never fall into the vulgar mistake of dreaming that I am persecuted whenever I am contradicted. ~ Ralph Waldo Emerson

Dedicated to

To those with Ears that Hear
And with Eyes that See

Masonic Biography of Walter L. Wilmshurst

Born June 22 1867

THE HUDDERSFIELD LODGE No. 290

Initiated December 11th, 1889

Passed January 8th, 1890

Raised February 5th, 1890

Steward 1891-1892

Registrar 1894-1895

Secretary 1896-1898

Resigned December 28th, 1898

PROSPERITY CHAPTER H.R.A., No. 290

Exalted February 11th, 1891

Resigned December 30th, 1898

THE LODGE OF HARMONY No. 275

Joined October 12th, 1899

Chaplain 1901

Registrar 1902-1903

J. W. 1908

W.M. 1909

LODGE OF LIVING STONES

Founder Master December 16th, 1927

W.M. 1928-1930 and 1937-1938

PROVINCE OF WEST YORKS

Prov. Grand Registrar 1913

Past Prov. Sen. Grand Warden 1926

GRAND LODGE

Past Asst. Grand D. of C. 1929

Died July 22 1939.

CONTENTS

MASONIC BIOGRAPHY OF WALTER L. WILMSHURST	XI
THE PRESENT ASPECT OF THE CONFLICT BETWEEN SCIENTIFIC AND RELIGIOUS THOUGHT	- 15 -
I - THE PARTING OF THE WAYS	- 15 -
REASON AND VISION	- 23 -
THE MYSTICAL BASIS OF MASONRY	- 33 -
THE HIDDEN CHURCH OF THE HOLY GRAAL	- 47 -
THE MYSTICAL IDEAL AS EXPRESSED IN POETRY	- 57 -
S. WINEFRIDE'S WELL AND LEGEND	- 67 -
I - The Well	- 67 -
SPURIOUS ECSTASY AND CEREMONIAL MAGIC	- 91 -
THE SECRET DOCTRINE IN ISRAEL	- 99 -
THE DEVELOPMENT OF THE CONFLICT	- 105 -
II - THE DEVELOPMENT OF THE CONFLICT	123 -
III - NEW FACTORS TENDING TO RECONCILIATION	128 -
IV - NEW FACTORS TENDING TO RECONCILIATION	134 -
V - THE PRESENT AND THE FUTURE	148 -
SCIENCE AND THE OCCULT AT THE BRITISH ASSOCIATION	- 161 -
AUTHOR AND MANAGING EDITOR	- 173 -
BOOKS BY THE MANAGING EDITOR	- 175 -
PORTRAITS AND ILLUSTRATIONS BY THE ARTIST	- 177 -

Walter L. Wilmshurst

THE PRESENT ASPECT OF THE CONFLICT BETWEEN SCIENTIFIC AND RELIGIOUS THOUGHT

And He made of one every nation of men,. . . having determined their appointed seasons,. . . that they should seek God if haply they might feel after Him and find Him,—though He is not far from each one of us. St. Paul.

So much more near than I had known, So much more great than I had guessed; An' me like all the rest,—alone, But reachin' out to all the rest. ~ Kipling.

I - THE PARTING OF THE WAYS

IN 1893, the present Prime Minister, speaking at a Royal Society dinner, used these words: "My friend Lord Kelvin has often talked to me of the future of Science. He has told me that to the man of science of today it appears as if we were trembling on the brink of some great scientific discovery which should give us a new view of the forces of Nature among which and in the midst of which we move." This peep into the private reflections of the greatest scientific mind since Sir Isaac Newton was a matter of much more than ordinary interest. As a Frenchman would say, it "gave one furiously to think." To the observant watcher of events the announcement was in the first place exciting, for it implied that at the end of a century, the richest upon record in the discovery of the processes of Nature, the foremost scientific genius of our time, who had lived through the longer part of that astonishing period, who from the pinnacle of his own great intellectual eminence had watched the gradual unfolding of the secret volume, and had himself, in ample measure, contributed both to the discoveries and to the practical application of some of the newly acquired knowledge to the service of his fellow men, seemed to regard these inestimable gains as but the prelude to a revelation in comparison with which they would pale into insignificance. And in the second place, it was disquieting; for past experience has taught us that any great revolution in the point of view from which we must look out upon the universe is liable to produce considerable reaction upon religious faith, and there is trouble until we grow used to the altered conditions.

Old ideas become upset; cherished preconceptions are dislocated; new demonstrations of science not squaring with ancient beliefs play havoc with both the private and the public conscience; scientific theory falls foul of religious dogma; and, our minds being probably made up and our convictions settled upon the deeper things of life, either we have to put up with an intellectual plant more or less old-fashioned, trusting that it will last out during our time, or else at some mental cost and pain throw it into the scrap-heap of worn-out ideas and formulate our views afresh. Take an illustration. Imagine the outlook upon the world of a Christian man 400 years ago. For him no principle was more settled, sure and irrefragable than that the earth was the center and chief fact of the Universe, that it was immovable, that it was flat, and that the sun and all the stars had been fashioned for the exclusive performance of certain functions for the convenience of man. For him, the Scriptures contained the sum of all knowledge and the authority of the Church discouraged any independent investigation of Nature. If by chance a passing interest was taken in some physical question, it was settled by a reference to the Bible or patristic literature, not by an appeal to phenomena. So great was the preference given to sacred over profane learning that

Christianity had been in existence for 1500 years without producing a single man of science in the ordinary acceptation of that term. Suddenly there came announcements tending to shake established ideas to the roots, and then began the conflict between scientific and religious thought which has waxed fiercer and fiercer until our own day.

To begin with, Ptolemy's old geographical scheme of the world with which men had been content for more than a dozen stay-at-home centuries, was shattered into bits by the prows of the tiny vessels with which Columbus lighted on his New World, by the doubling of the Cape of Good Hope and the opening of a sea route to the east by De Gama, and by the triumphant circumnavigation of the globe from west to east by Magellan. When the San Vittoria dropped anchor near Seville in 1522 after her three years voyage, the theological doctrine of the flatness of the earth was irretrievably overthrown. The scientific reasoning of three sailors had, in twenty years, upset the faith of fifteen centuries in regard to the form and size of the earth. In another twenty years, a still more momentous announcement was forthcoming, respecting its position with regard to the sun and the planetary bodies. Copernicus, amid the denunciations of the Church, propounded the heliocentric theory.

He showed that the earth is a mere point in the heavens, revolving round the sun, which itself with its concomitant planets, is wheeling at inconceivable speed, through ghastly vacuities of space, among other sidereal systems compared with some of which ours is a trifle. Then indeed were the vials of orthodox wrath opened. What happened is a familiar story. Time has withered most of the romance out of it, but the imagination will always interest itself in contemplating the history of the days when natural science first ran at full tilt against religious authority. It is almost impossible now to realize the dismay, the disquietude and the anxiety with which such a proposition must have been listened to 400 years ago. We, living in an age of discovery, instead of being lost in wonder at new disclosures, have almost lost our wonder altogether, and can hardly realize the effect that must have been produced upon a thinking mind four centuries ago by scientific revelations which displaced all previous ideas of man's place in the Universe; affected, apparently, the relationship between him and his Maker, and plied him with many obstinate and pitiless questionings. To dethrone the earth from her central dominating position, to give her many equals and not a few superiors, seemed to diminish her claims upon the divine regard. If each of the countless myriads of stars was a sun, surrounded by revolving globes peopled with responsible beings like ourselves; if we had fallen so easily and had been redeemed at so stupendous a price as the death of the Son of God. How was it with them? Of them were there, none who had fallen or might fall like us? Where, then, for them could a Savior be found? Thus was cast the first shadow of doubt and skepticism upon the pages of Holy Writ wherein were contained not only the law and the gospel to guide man's faith and morals, but also, as was supposed, whatsoever things were true and worthy to be believed in matters of natural science.

The establishment of the heliocentric theory, then, was the first great achievement won by natural science at the expense of theological teaching. Propounded by Copernicus, it came to be established by the astronomical researches of Galileo, Tycho Brahe, and Kepler. The Church fought against the heresy with all the furious vengeance of the Inquisition and the Index. It imprisoned Galileo; it murdered Bruno. The truth it could not kill. Then, fortunately for everyone, occurred the Reformation, securing comparative liberty of thought and weakening many of the old ecclesiastical bonds. Under its liberal influence occurred the next great epoch not only in European science but in the intellectual development of man. Newton, *with his prism and silent face Voyaging through strange seas of thought alone,* presented the world with the "Principia," confirming the pronouncements of his astronomical predecessors, and establishing the theory of gravitation. The "Principia" established for the first time the presence of the operation of law in the physical universe. It not only accepted the heliocentric theory but showed it to be a mathematical necessity, and demonstrated the impossibility of things being other than they are; that the solar and starry systems are not, as ecclesiastical authority alleged, brought into existence by arbitrary fiats and controlled by periodical providential interventions, but are under the government of irreversible law—of law that is the issue of mathematical necessity.

The outcome of Newton's teaching was the development of the nebular hypothesis of Laplace, which explains, upon the basis of the perpetual operation of law, the genesis, progress and decay of the members of the sidereal systems. Upon this hypothesis is based the whole fabric of modern astronomy. It stands in direct conflict with all that ecclesiastical authority held true as to the creation of the earth. In the light of it, the literal construction of the first chapter of Genesis, which theretofore had been the sole explanation of the creation of the world, led to palpable untruth. In the place of the creative fiat of the Deity, bidding this world and starry firmament suddenly to be, it disclosed that going on through illimitable space was a mechanical process by which nebulous gaseous mists coalesce into vast masses of matter at a temperature of incandescence; that cooling and radiation are necessary incidents; that the nebulae break up into fragmentary planets with a decline of heat and form themselves into organized solar systems, such as that of which we form a part, and that they eventually lose heat, decay, and become destroyed. So far had astronomical science come into conflict with the Scriptural cosmogony. But other sciences came forward to reinforce the conclusions of astronomy.

Geology and paleontology furnished evidence of the far greater antiquity of the earth and of man than Scripturalists taught; biology accounted for the development of organic life of every type by a far different method than that of special creation offered by the Bible. The doctrine of the fall of man, which was the very bedrock of the Christian scheme of salvation, was met point blank by evidence of the rise of man from sources much humbler than his present state. The converging testimony of a score of distinct departments of knowledge pointed to a principle underlying all organic and inorganic nature—the principle of evolution. There are lacunae in the chain of knowledge, the most conspicuous being the gap, yet to be bridged, between inorganic matter and living organisms. But the cumulative evidence in favor of the evolutionary process from the lowest form of matter to matter charged with and exhibiting the highest functioning's of mind is well-nigh irresistible. From the nebula to the gaseous sun, from the sun to the separated planet, from the molten planetary mass to the vaporous and solidifying stages, from the decomposition and rearrangement of particles of inorganic matter to the germination of rudimentary life, from the simple organism to the complex, from the brute to man, from barbaric man to civilized and social man, from the homogeneous to the heterogeneous in every department and phase of existence; such was found to be the process of creation

From harmony to harmony this universal world began, When Nature underneath a heap of jarring atoms lay ... Then cold and hot and moist and dry in order to their stations leaped.. . . From harmony to harmony, this universal world began; Through all the compass of the notes it ran, The diapason closing full in Man.

Thus did the muse of Dryden anticipate the conclusions of modern Science. To sum up; the teeming discoveries of modern natural science have resulted in the formulation of three fundamental principles,

> "Already in Germany have inorganic and artificial substances been found to crawl about on glass slides under the action of surface-tension or capillarity, with an appearance which is said to have deceived even a biologist into hastily pronouncing them living amoeba. Life in its ultimate element and on its material side is such a simple thing; it is but a slight extension of known chemical and physical forces. . . . I apprehend there is not a biologist but believes (perhaps quite erroneously) that sooner or later the discovery will be made and that a cell having all the essential functions of life will be constructed out of inorganic material."

which, so far as can be seen, must be rooted for ever as cardinal concepts in our apprehension of the Universe; principles to which all ecclesiastical teaching, whatever else it may inculcate, must henceforth conform. They are these: (1) The presence of Law, operating in a diversity of ways, but persistently, not sporadically, throughout the Universe. (2) Creation by means of Evolution, a perennial process operating *Nunc, semper et ubique* **(Now, always and everywhere)** by means of gradual development and selection; as opposed to creation by arbitrary fiat and instantaneous manifestation. (3) The existence of the Ether, a tenuous fluid embracing the whole Universe and uniting its parts into (so to speak) solidity; saturating its minutest atomic constituents, making our world brother to the remotest stars and one with interstellar space; (a sublime conception which, by demonstrating the earth's relation to the All, invalidates the idea of its comparative insignificance when measured by the scale of cosmic vastness). The crowning achievement of the nineteenth century is to have ascertained and formulated these fundamental principles of the objective Universe. And now at the end of it, with this tremendous addition to our stock of knowledge, and after we have been obliged to reformulate our ideas upon the majority of matters, we are told in "bated breath and whispering humbleness" by the most eminent of our scientists that after all we are trembling on the brink of some further great discovery that shall give us a new view of the forces of Nature! What will that discovery reveal? Past experience tells us it will disclose something lying very close to us, sealed from us only by our ignorance or the undeveloped state of our faculties; that it will be some important factor in the mechanism of the Universe of which we are at present unconscious, but which all the time is.

REASON AND VISION

THERE are two paths by which the human mind endeavors to approach the sanctuary of ultimate truth. The first, the more general, and, as it eventually proves, the inadequate method, is that of reason; ordered, calculated thought, based upon objective evidence and drawing its conclusions from within the limits of individual experience and from such phenomena as are found available. The faculty employed in this case is the rationalizing intellect, which, as it works, enacts its own laws of logic and evidence, and formulates its own canons and criteria of judgment, thereby necessarily restricting its own capacities and conclusions to its own self-forged fetters. A formidable query-mark therefore always stands opposite the results of the rationalistic method, for, firstly, the quantum of experience varies with individual minds, and, secondly, the laws of logic applicable to one man's measure of experience are apt to break down when applied to another's. Follow the track of pure reason far enough and it leads to a position altogether impracticable and inconsistent with your own or someone else's personal experience. Again, we have schools of both materialistic and of idealistic philosophy, and (to leave the former entirely out of account in the present consideration) the official professors of the latter are found to be seriously disunited in their conclusions. Does ultimate, perfected truth already exist? They ask; is it something static and directly cognizable, or still in the process of making? Are things moving towards an assured "divine event," or towards something undetermined and in *futuro*, the nature of which depends upon the way in which the totality of cosmic forces develop? Is Deity already fully extant and in control of the universe or still only coming to birth concurrently with the universal evolutionary processes?

Are there intermediate "lords many and gods many"? Is there an Absolute behind, encircling all? Even if monotheists, are we logically bound to be monists? Are there not strong reasons for being dualists, and still stronger ones for being pluralists?

So far, and into such perplexities do reason and its organ the logical intellect, even when committed to a spiritualistic view of things, lead us. The alternative and rarer method of approaching the final verities is by means of a faculty quite other than the reason, and indeed one in regard to which reason stands in constant conflict. It involves a direct act or state of consciousness which places the individual, though he touches but the hem of its garment, in first-hand relation with what he realizes irrefutably to be a permanent Reality forming the woof of both himself and all else. Greek philosophy defined this faculty as the "active reason" as opposed to the "passive reason" or "carnal mind"; it is "the Knower" of Oriental *religio*-philosophy; it cognizes rather than intellectualizes; and it is, in fact, the only true and reliable organ of knowledge we possess. That it may be abused or allowed to act ill-regulatedly is as unquestioned as that a ship's engines will "race" when the propeller they drive becomes lifted above the water it is intended to work in. But given a duly balanced human organism, it is the intuitive faculty that should control and inspire the reason, whereas the reverse method usually prevails, and the subordinate faculty is allowed to usurp the throne and dispossess the rightful king.

Thus it ensues, that the value of any man's philosophy depends more upon the measure of his illumination than upon that of his intellectual power. "Where there is no vision, the people perisheth." Excess of intellectualism produces an inadequate philosophy; illuminated reason alone can show us any good. As the Welsh mystic Thomas Vaughan quaintly puts it, "It is a terrible thing to prefer Aristotle to the Elohim." Now the present position of the official philosophy taught in the academies of learning, and of which one phase is exhibited in Professor W. James's recent Gifford Lectures just issued under the title of "A Pluralistic Universe", is extremely interesting and suggestive, because many of its exponents, if not yet arrived at the summit of the mount of vision, seem assuredly to be traversing the lower slopes that lead thereto. This brightest and breeziest of philosophers realizes fully the value of transcendental experience as distinct from mere intellectualism. "A man's vision is the great fact about him," he declares, not his reasons; and since "philosophy is essentially the vision of things seen from above," the wider the range of a man's consciousness, the greater the value to us of both himself and his philosophy.

It is then from the standpoint of empiricism—that is, from the experiences of personal consciousness—that Professor James embarks upon a journey of protest against the monistic idealism obtaining in modem seats of philosophic learning. Briefly, his argument is this. An idealistic view of the universe may involve the following beliefs: (1) a dualistic theism, postulating God and man over against each other, a view which "makes us outsiders and keeps us foreigners to God.... His action can affect us, but He can never be affected by our reaction; ... not heart of our heart and reason of our reason, but our magistrate rather"; and (2) a pantheism involving intimacy between man and the creative principle, with which we may consider ourselves substantially one; "the divine, the most intimate of all our possessions; heart of our heart, in fact." But this pantheistic belief can itself be subdivided into two forms: one, which conceives "that the divine exists authentically only when the world is experienced all at once, in its absolute totality" (which, it is urged, may never be actually experienced or realized in that shape at all); and another, which holds that an Absolute may not at present exist, and that "a disseminated, distributed, or incompletely unified appearance is the only form reality may yet have achieved."

It is this latter idea that Professor James champions at length; one that assumes a plurality of consciousness's as against a divine mono-consciousness; one that, he claims, whilst making of God one of many conscious beings "affords the greater degree of intimacy" for us. For the ideally perfect Whole is one of which the parts are also perfect; but alas, we, the parts, are imperfect; hence, if the world is, as it appears to be, still incomplete and unfinished, instead of believing in one Absolute Reality, is it not more rational to conceive reality as existing distributively, not yet in an All, but in a set of eaches, or pluralistically? But even if the idea of an Absolute is dropped, is there no consciousness better than our own? Yes; "the tenderer parts of personal life are continuous with a more of the same quality operative in the universe outside us and with which we may keep in working touch; . . . we are continuous, to our own consciousness at any rate, with a wider self from which saving experiences flow in." And here, because of such experiences, which reason would never have inferred in advance of their actual coming, but which, as they actually do come and are given, cause creation to widen to the view of the recipients, the Professor finds himself obliged to break away from logic and intellectualism and stands ranged, in a quite literal sense, upon the side of the angels.

The impetus of his own argument leads him to a belief, similar to that held by the late German psychologist Fechner, in a pluralistic pan-psychic universe teeming with superhuman life with which, unknown to ourselves, we are co-conscious; "angels and men ordained and constituted in a wonderful order," as the old Church collect has it. In so far as the Professor's treatise speculates upon the finiteness or otherwise of Deity, of whom he claims we are indeed internal parts and not external creations, it may strike one as but ungrand *peut-être*. Apparently, he claims no more for it, nor needs the problem to vex even the most susceptible religious mind. To know even dimly the God of this world is all that men of this world need to know; and that there are still higher, and as yet undeclared, heights are not improbable in a universe whereof our world is but a grain of dust, nor are some forms of religion without warrants for such a supposition. But the significance of this doctrine at the present era of intellectual reconstruction is that it constrains rationalism henceforward to recognize that fullness of life exceeds the limits of logic by taking into account the experiences of the mystical consciousness and by furnishing a rationale for belief in those vast orders and hierarchies of intelligences transcending our own which Milton's famous line summarizes as—"Thrones, Dominations, Princedoms, Virtues, Powers," and which, under various names, are common to every theosophical system. And though with these we may as yet be disconnected in consciousness, yet this pluralistic universe, it is claimed, is self-reparative through ourselves, as getting its disconnections remedied in part by our behavior. Truly a high and noble motive for human conduct.

Dr. Rufus Jones' Studies in Mystical Religion, a substantial and admirably written volume from another American Professor, gives us a compilation of just those experiences upon which Professor James bases his hope for the future of both philosophy and religion. Again, how significant is the present day demand for the literature of mysticism and for what Dr. Jones calls "initiation into the Divine Secret"; betokening both a reaction from rationalism and a protest against the insufficiency of orthodox doctrine. An aphorism in Mr. A.E. Waite's Steps to the Crown asserts that "The consolation of God is in His mystics rather than in His angels"; which sounds daring until one reflects that today the consolation of men also seems to be in the mystics and the literature concerning them rather than in the official schools and churches, and that in this as in many respects *quod inferius sicut est quod superius* **(As we mentioned above and below)**. Dr. Jones' book being in the nature of a historical record tracing Christian mysticism from its roots in Platonism and classical literature down to the seventeenth century, there is perhaps nothing new in it for those familiar with the subject and with its exponents. Its virtue lies in the skillful collation and presentation he has made from many scattered records of the experiences and testimony of men and women forming "a continuous prophetical procession; a mystical brotherhood, through the centuries, of those who have lived by the soul's immediate vision."

In respect of a book of over 500 well-filled pages, written with obvious sympathy and insight and with both historical and philosophical learning, we shall not complain if he has not exhausted his subject, especially as he promises a further volume to be devoted exclusively to that master-mystic Jacob Boehme and states that the present is but an introduction to a series of historical volumes by himself and others devoted to the development and spiritual environment of a particular branch of Christianity, the Society of Friends. What is given to us is excellent, notably the introductory chapter on "The Nature and Value of First-Hand Experience in Religion," in which he defines mysticism as "the type of religion which puts the emphasis on immediate awareness of relation with God; on direct and intimate consciousness of the Divine Presence. It is religion in its most acute, intense and living stage."

For those desiring a compendium of excerpts and mystical testimony from primitive and Alexandrian Christianity, from Montanism, Neo-Platonism, the Waldenses, the Franciscans, and numerous Brotherhood groups, or from the memorials of such great names as Augustine, Dionysius, John Scotus, Eckhart, Suso, Ruysbroek, and others down to George Fox, no more useful or impartial collection can be recommended. Now, totally unlike that of the professional rationalists, the testimony of this innumerable cloud of witnesses, from the saint upon the mount of contemplation to the itinerant preaching Quaker, is uniform, and it is certain. Their expression may vary with the fashion of their time or be tinctured by the intellectual environment of their age, but all testify to having had contact with and drawn upon one "matrix consciousness" wider than their natural selves, and all affirm that nothing can hinder anyone from rising to the divine union if he but puts forth the will to rise. "Their testimony to unseen Realities," says Dr. Jones, "gives the clue and stimulus to multitudes of others to gain a like experience, and it is, too, their testimony that makes God real to the great mass of men who are satisfied to believe on the strength of another's belief."

The series of volumes, then, which this one inaugurates cannot but perform a great service as well in the interest of personal religion as in that of general history, and we accord to it our most sincere commendation. By many tokens, including books such as these under review, proceeding though they do upon different but converging lines, it appears that we are at length moving away from an age of speculation and reason towards one of—at least, the desire for—intimacy with realities. And this advance accords, no doubt, with the cosmic order of development; "first that which is natural, afterwards that which is spiritual." Intellectualism is beginning to readjust its functions to its appropriate limits so that a greater light than itself may be revealed. The mystics, persecuted, despised and rejected for centuries, are at last coming into their own, and are bringing sheaves of others with them.

These followers of the inward way have constituted hitherto but a slender minority, but that minority is now coming to be recognized as having been the saving salt of the earth. With one voice, they have testified to one truth and to one experience. They have risen superior to the methods of logic and to the academies of learning; they have transcended the letter and the formulae of official theological doctrine. Around them human life has come and gone in millions of legions, and but for them the long centuries have passed darkly. Can any progress be said to have occurred in the apprehension of things ultimate on the part of those who chose the broader path; the outward, intellectual way? It is doubtful. Possibly some slight elevation of the intellectual order has taken place, an advance commensurate with the development, since primitive times, of cranial capacity and brain-surface, if any value can derive from such a merely physical increase. Doubtless, the range of intellectual vision has been widened, though it has often been darkened, by the revelations of physical science; some obscure places have been clarified a little, and a store of concrete facts has been garnered, constituting for future generations a patrimony that will obviate the need of discovering and relearning everything *da capo*. But, after all, such advance is but quantitative, not qualitative; all it amounts to is a widening, not a deepening, of knowledge.

Knowledge is no guarantee of sanctity and avails little until it is transmuted into wisdom; its mere widening tends to stupefy and paralyze the mind rather than to illumine it. "He that increaseth knowledge, increaseth sorrow." No man ever won to the heights or lifted the veil of Isis by bigness, and coordinating grasp of brain merely. No; for every newborn life the old riddles recur in all their primal perplexity. To every soul upon entering this earthly prison-house, the water of Lethe is given to drink. It forgets its own nature, and its native faculties become temporarily abrogated. Its eyes are bandaged by the veil of mortality which permits it but that substituted method of vision which we call human reason; and no matter who has previously passed this way, or what others may have divined before it in humanity's great hall of initiation and testing, it still remains the personal private task of each of us to pluck out the heart of the mystery for himself. But let a man turn inwards and seek to rend the veil of his own temple from top to bottom; let him lift the hoodwink of reason that blinds his power of interior vision; let him bare the burnished mirror of his inward self to that unquenchable intra-cosmic Light which illuminates and alone makes possible all lesser lights whether of the physical, intellectual, or moral order, and there will open for him, and within him, what Russell Lowell has finely called—"The soul's east window of divine surprise," and once and for all he will pass beyond the vexation of merely intellectual pseudo-problems; beyond the region of theological controversy and philosophic speculation; and to all protests and challenges of objecting critics, he will answer and persistently affirm," One thing I know; that whereas before I was blind, now I see."

Walter L. Wilmshurst

THE MYSTICAL BASIS OF MASONRY

WHEN, in 1646, the founder of the Ashmolean Library recorded that he had been made a Freemason at Warrington, or when, some five decades later, the architects, contractors and superintendents of works engaged upon the reconstruction of the metropolitan cathedral foregathered after their day's work in masonic assemblies of another character at the Goose and Gridiron Tavern in St. Paul's Churchyard, no one was likely to have foreseen that during the ensuing two centuries, and out of the then exiguous community of Freemasons, the enormous Masonic organization that now flourishes in our midst would have sprung into being.

At the present moment, holding warrants from the central authority—the Grand Lodge of England—alone, there exist roughly some three thousand Masonic Lodges with an estimated aggregate membership of 150,000. The Scottish and Irish divisions of Great Britain work under separate constitutions of their own but upon similar lines to the English, whilst the British dependencies, the United States and every other civilized country in the world, with the exception of Japan, contain Masonic organizations, the total membership of which constitutes a great multitude which there is no opportunity of numbering, and which is annually increasing. It is thus obvious that the Masonic idea has caught and continues to hold a firm grip upon the imaginations of a very considerable body of humanity and that distinction of race and language has proved no bar to a universal appreciation of it.

The inwardness of the phenomenon passes unobserved even within the Masonic community itself, although the external fact of the diffusion of the Masonic system throughout the world is, of course, not merely notorious, but is one of which large and agreeable advantage is taken by members of the Fraternity, and it may be profitable to accord a brief consideration to it here and to inquire what is the secret of the wide appeal Freemasonry has made during the last couple of centuries and still continues to make.

The problem is doubtless very complex, and to the question proposed a variety of offhand answers might be tendered, the value of which would depend largely upon the perspicuity of the respondent and his friendliness, or the reverse, towards the Masonic system. That system provides occasion for social, fraternal—and, to meet the claims of the cynic, I will add—convivial, intercourse amongst a number of individuals who choose to segregate themselves into a distinctive fraternity with no deeper purpose than this is, one may reasonably submit, an incredible motive to justify an organization so firmly entrenched, so robust and associated with such personalities of eminence and character as have been formerly or still are actively connected with it. That it is an instrument for furthering practical benevolence and philanthropy, which it certainly does and does handsomely, is a similarly inadequate pretext; Masonry was not intended to be, and is not, a high-grade Friendly Society and its charitable energies are merely an incident of, and not the motive for, its existence. That it is a school of morality, tending to promote peace and goodwill amongst men, which is also wholly true, again fails to suffice, for men need not join a secret society, or enter into the obligations of silence required therefrom, merely to learn rudimentary ethics which it is the common duty of the whole world to know and practice. That it is, as is not infrequently alleged, an engine for promoting the mutual temporal aggrandizement of its members to the prejudice of non-members; a cover for political intrigue, or a screen for propagating antireligious ideas, are again idle suspicions. That political or other intrigues have in the past been conducted—as in connection with the pretensions of the Jacobite's and Legitimists in both England and France in times of revolution—under the *aegis* of societies claiming to be Masonic, is doubtless a fact; but this, when established, proves merely that a fraud has been committed upon a system devoted to entirely different purposes. Speaking for British Masonry today, it is as innocent of such purposes as a mother's meeting and, indeed, is wholly untinctured with even the political partisanship manifested, whether passively or actively, by the official churches of the land; whilst the notorious ban of the Roman Church upon the Masonic brotherhood as being a trespass against the exclusive spiritual and temporal rights of the former is, upon a moment's reflection, stultified by that Church's own insidious political record.

By an eliminative process, then, we arrive at the sole remaining *raison d'etre* for the spread and attractiveness of the Masonic system, namely, the significance and implications involved within its ceremonial rites. Now if these, or some subtly-speaking voice in these, be not, when all irrelevant and accretionary consideration have been removed, the fundamental essence and the secret of the vitality and the development of Masonry, there remains no justification for its existence worthy of account. It matters not that in the case of a large majority of the Fraternity that voice is not a loud one or that the significance of its purport is but dimly recognized; and it may be admitted that among Masons themselves there are but few who have entered into a full intellectual realization of their own heritage. The fact remains that something veiled, latent and deep down in those rites speaks to something that is latent and responsive, however faintly, in those who participate in them; some remote *causa causans*, apart from the mere impressiveness and solemnity of the rites themselves, which for most remains unrealized and unformulated in the consciousness, but which, nevertheless, induces those who partake in them to feel that they are in the presence of a mystery that goes to the root of their being and that it is good for them to be there.

Walter L. Wilmshurst

To what element in the Masonic rites, then, is to be traced to the effectiveness and subtlety of the appeal alluded to? Among the Fraternity, as well as among the outside public, there are many who, in the absence of better information, suppose Masonry to be a system of immemorial antiquity, one which, for some undefined reason or another, became instituted for no very definite object among primitive inhabitants of the East, and which for some equally indefinite purpose it is still desirable to perpetuate in the West. It is supposed also that the predecessors of the present Craft were concerned in operative building and erected, among other edifices of both earlier and later date, the national Temple of Israel at Jerusalem traditionally associated with the name of King Solomon. To dissipate the misconceptions inherent in these suppositions, to dematerialize the outward veils and exhibit the inward and real significance of the matter, would take me far beyond the limits permitted to the present paper. It is a fact of the commonest knowledge that systems of initiation into certain spiritual secrets and mysteries have obtained immemorially; it is doubtless true that guilds and trade-unions of operative builders possessing also elementary rites, secret signs, tokens, and privileges of membership, flourished from very remote epochs and subsisted until comparatively recent times; it is the fact also that at least the superiors and chief architects connected with such communities were profoundly instructed, as the fanes and monuments of the past and the great cathedrals of Christendom attest, in the principles of deep-reaching symbolism, and that with consecrated minds and reverent hands they introduced those principles into the construction of religious edifices by way of emblematizing in stone the perfect temple man should build in his mind and body if ultimately he is to participate in another temple that is eternal and not built with hands. But this is far from saying that modern Masonry is the perpetuation, or the faithful, lineal image, either of ancient mystery-systems or of the operative masonic communities, though doubtless points of

Forgotten Essays

JACQUES DE MOLAY (1240-1314).

connection with both survive. Every Mason knows that his Craft purports to initiate into certain secrets and mysteries; every Mason knows that in that system the tools, tackle and terminology of operative masons are employed; but a moment's reflection will tell him that the secrets and mysteries referred to are not those of any industrial trade (which, of course, can have none of other than commercial value); that the incidents of the operative trade have been merely used as the outward apparel within which to clothe truths of a moral and spiritual order; and lastly that the chief of the Craft degrees—that which embodies its great and central legend or traditional history, and as a preparation for instruction in which the antecedent degrees are, in theory, processes of purification—is devoted, from the first word of its opening to the last of its closing, to the veiled presentation of something which, upon the one hand, is as unassociated with mundane architecture as the east is distant from the west, but which, upon the other, is an integral factor and root element of every system of religious initiation of antiquity.

In modem speculative Masonry, then, is to be traced a confluence of two distinct systems. Some time in the seventeenth century the elementary rites of membership used till then among the then virtually obsolete operative guilds became taken over, under circumstances now very obscure and by individuals almost equally so, and adapted to serve as the vehicle for the expression of a highly mystical and *religio*-philosophic doctrine disconnected altogether from mundane architecture and unrelated to any form of masonry other than that which, by employing metaphor, we may call the building—or perhaps the rebuilding and reintegration—of that uncompleted temple, the human soul.

It may be stated at this point that the credit of reaching the conclusion just mentioned is attributable wholly to Mr. A. E. Waite, who first gave voice to it in some illuminative papers in his Studies in Mysticism and added some confirmatory words in his subsequent book, *The Hidden Church of the Holy Graal*. The facts involved in the conclusion had previously escaped the observation of historians of Masonry, who speaking perhaps without any, and certainly without Mr. Waite's extensive knowledge of the movements in occultism and mysticism that were occurring behind the scenes of public history in Europe and England during the past few centuries, have been without adequate equipment for tracing the real genesis of modem Masonry. It is notorious that at, and for long prior to, that genesis in this country and the continent were alive with occultists and initiates—of pretensions both meritorious and the reverse—connected with schools of alchemy, magic, *Rosicrucianism* and what not. The worthy name and written remains of Thomas Vaughan alone, apart from the wide testimony of contemporaneous literature to the prevalence of occult inquiry, testify that earnest students and genuine adepts were in the field at the date of the inception of the Masonic movement, and it is reasonable to deduce a connection between these and the movement itself. In the old operative system, they, or some of them, found, as it were, a body prepared; they imported into that body a new spirit and gave it a transfigured life, a life which, in its maturer growth, is with us in such magnitude today. To use an expression of Mr. Waite's, "they made an experiment upon the mind of the age," and, be it remembered, it was an experiment made, and perhaps made with shrewd insight and foresight, at the commencement of an epoch when the tide of spiritual life and understanding in the official churches was about to run extremely low and the tide of rationalistic thought and scientific materialism to rise extremely high, and when, maybe, it was found desirable, for the benefit of a few in the dark days that were to follow, to kindle a new beacon-light testifying to a truth and a doctrine that have never been absent from the world.

It being my purpose in this article to bespeak the attention alike of those who are technically Masons and of those who are not to a further and extremely valuable work upon the esoteric development and mystical aspect of Masonry and its numerous ramifications and allied rites, the foregoing considerations may perhaps not be misplaced, since their intention is to clear the somewhat befogged atmosphere in which the true history and vital purpose of the

Masonic system have become involved in both the Masonic and the public mind. In the volumes referred to—and they deal not with the external and virtually negligible history of Masonry, but with its interior content, its mystical purport and its place in the long chain of occult tradition—Mr. Waite demonstrates after what manner Masonry, in both its Craft and High Grades and its cognate rites, is an expression, perhaps far from a full, but still an indubitable, one, of that Secret Tradition which throughout all time has been perpetuated with the object of instructing those that were keenly enough concerned with solving the riddle of existence to consent to adopt the methods which that Tradition accredits and guarantees. The quest after that solution is for ever proceeding, amongst however few. We n ay call it the quest of the Graal; we may call it the search for the Lost Word, or the guarding of an empty Sepulcher; we may term it the achievement of the Great Work, or the discovery of the Philosopher's Stone; or we may refer to it in the terms of the Platonist as the task of reintegrating the divine element in man with the Divine Basis of the Universe. The systems have been many, but the quest, and the goal of the quest, are but one. Many of these systems, expressed sometimes in terms of baffling ingenuity lest the pearls they contain should fall into unworthy hands, have long since passed away, to be replaced by others. Like the ever-renewed branches of the Tree of Life—*uno avulso non deficit alter aureus* **(in one he cuts off, another golden one does not fail)**; when one has served its day another has manifested without fail, as if (but is it not part of the Tradition that it is so?) there was watching over Israel—the small, but continuous body of dedicated, undaunted aspirants—that which slumbers not nor sleeps; a watch of unseen wardens whose concern is to keep ever open and illumined the pathway to that Center whereto all experience leads and wherein all quests end.

Mr. Waite defines the Secret Tradition as (1) the memorials of a cosmic loss which has befallen humanity, and (2) the records of a restitution in respect of that which is lost. It is innermost knowledge concerning man's way of return whence he came, by a method of inward life. But, by a paradox, that method of inward life is also one of inward death. There has been no accredited system of mystery-teaching but has proclaimed, whether in legend, symbol, or dramatic representation, the fact that death, interpreted in a mystical sense, is the gate of that life which is not merely post-mortem existence, but conscious, irrefragable union with the Eternal Basis of the Universe. It may be urged, and with truth, that this doctrine is, or was intended to be, that of official public religion. I am not concerned here to discuss to what extent the churches have conveyed or failed to convey this truth in its plenitude to the consciousness of their adherents, and I am far from asserting that the collateral Masonic system can claim an advantage in this respect. But there is none among the millions who have received the degree of Master-Mason but may reflect that not only has he symbolically undergone an experience which has been the crux and center of all the great Mystery-schools of the past, but that in so doing he has in his own person testified to a truth which is inherent in the moral fabric of the Cosmos itself. And herein lies the peculiar purpose and value of ceremonial initiation as against systems that are but didactic or mainly so. The doctrine imparted is given an

Louis Claude de Saint-Martin (1743-1803).

Louis Claude De Saint Martin

immediately personal application. The imagination of the disciple is intended to be impressed through his being identified with, and made to enact ceremonially, that which it is essential for him to learn, to the intent that thereafter he may in his own life and consciousness become that which he has sacramentally portrayed.

Such being the nature and purpose of arcane rites, Mr. Waite, who appears to be in the probably exceptional position of being personally familiar with the entire range of those now extant, as well as with the records of many now in desuetude, has been enabled in this book to apply his well-known qualifications as a mystic to collating them and assessing their respective values; a laborious task conducted with unfailing skill and tact, for in dealing with matters to which covenants of privacy attach he has been confronted upon one side with the difficulty of avoiding saying things to which those obligations would apply, and, upon the other, with that of saying too little to render an important subject intelligible to the non-Masonic inquirer. This twofold problem he has effectually surmounted. Faithful in respect of those matters which are the private prescriptions of secret communities, he has been abundantly generous in his exposition of those which exceed the range of all the instituted systems and can never become the monopoly of any since they are open to humanity at large. For this reason, although those who are officially Masons will, in virtue of their inside knowledge, stand at an advantage, the book need in no sense be deemed as restricted to their consideration, but is meant for a far wider public. The Mason of whatever rank will receive from it an illumination perhaps little suspected as possible in regard to his own science, which is now, and for the first time, subjected to an exegesis never hitherto undertaken; whilst the non-Mason who may be interested no less than his initiated brother in the development of mystical knowledge and philosophy, and the forms in which these have found expression from time to time, will find ample scope for profitable instruction and reflection.

Space does not avail here for detailed reference to the contents of Mr. Waite's book, or to the interesting collection of illustrations of cryptic symbols and of portraits of some of those who have been conspicuously associated with the expression and transmission of mystical doctrine and rites, and of which a few are here reproduced. The two volumes themselves constitute an extremely handsome setting to a unique work which, as a Mason myself, I most gratefully welcome and commend to my brethren and all others whom it may concern as the most important contribution to Masonic literature that has hitherto appeared. I have preferred in this notice of it to limit myself to emphasizing a conviction of its value and to indicating the fact that it must need mark an epoch in the history of a system which has developed as it were from a mustard-seed until it has overgrown the whole earth. Masonry in some at least of its grades may be, as Mr. Waite shows, an imperfect expression of the Secret Tradition, and the average Mason may, and doubtless does, enter into but an incomplete understanding of the full content of his system even as imperfectly expressed, although reasonable excuses for his so doing might perhaps be advanced. But the present work should make such excuses henceforth impermissible, and for this reason, it may be destined in time to assist in transforming and elevating the whole conscience and motive of the Masonic body. In a system which hitherto, with so intangible and obscure a reason, has developed as Masonry already has done there, he, now that the reason is unveiled and a new motive is displayed, enormous possibilities; and in this regard I am thinking less of its future numerical strength than of the augmented spiritual stature of its adherents. Masonry may yet become an undreamed of power for good, especially when regard is had to the increasing decadence of the churches and the vapidity of their teaching. Connected with its future is the problem, already becoming urgent, of the admission of women, against which there is, of course, no *a priori* or other substantial objection.

The natural conservatism inherent in vested interests and arising from long usage may eventually dissolve when a fuller realization of what is involved is attained. Upon the continent a few lodges are opening their doors to women, whilst the Co-Masonic movement working in connection with the Theosophical Society already numbers some dozen lodges admitting both sexes. Of this latter movement Mr. Waite speaks somewhat impatiently, but rather because of its reputed supervision by an elusive entity described as the Comte de Saint Germain than from prejudice against feminine rights to participate in mystical rites and philosophy. In the words of the apostle-initiate, the man is not without the woman, nor the woman without the man, in the Divine Idea, and, besides abundant precedents from antiquity, there are good warrants for associating them together in any system whose ultimate goal is the conscious realization of that Idea. There was once, it may be remembered, a building which, through the mouth of a great prophet, was rejected and condemned by the Great Architect because it had been "daubed with untempered mortar."

My references to Masonry in this article are, like Mr. Waite's book, not meant to be restricted merely to the Craft grades and their extension, the Royal Arch; they extend to Masonic grades and cognate rites lying beyond these, and some of them are entirely beyond the range of the average Mason's present vision. Those whose existence is a matter of public knowledge are, as Mr. Waite observes, analogous to what in former days were known as the Lesser Mysteries. But as beyond these there subsisted the more withdrawn and Greater Mysteries for those who were proficient and well equipped, so also, we are assured in these volumes, the corresponding form of the latter is amidst us today. It is of the Masonic method and the initiatory system as a whole that I have written, and if in what is here said I have done less than justice to the important volumes under notice, the deficiency is due to a desire to exhibit in the space at my disposal the standpoint from which they should be read. They form the greatest contribution in the way of expository literature that Masonry has received. It remains now with the Masonic Fraternity—and with doubtless many eager inquirers outside of it—to take advantage of them and to enlarge their borders of understanding in regard to a momentous and underestimated subject.

Walter L. Wilmshurst

THE HIDDEN CHURCH OF THE HOLY GRAAL

WHAT was, and is, the Holy Graal? Not to waste space in considering fatuous imaginings concerning any material reliquary that may once have served at a certain sacred feast and was supposed subsequently to have been concealed at Glastonbury or elsewhere, be it remembered that there has obtained no extensive or important system of religious expression, whether ethnic or Christian, but has instinctively formulated the conception of a feeding-dish communicating supernatural food; a cauldron brimming with some celestial brew; a cornucopia, bowl, or horn of plenty, exuberant with luscious fruits; each the symbol of that mystical, invisible, but unfailing cup or platter from which the inward life of man is, by all save those unconscious of an inward life, felt to be sustained. The Holy Graal is the gracious Christianized form of this catholic symbol. Besides the cup itself, it involves also the content of the cup; the Sangreal, or sacred vessel, as if language itself refused to dissociate the inward content from the outward vehicle, is also the *Sang Réal*, the Royal Blood, or life-giving Spirit, imparted therefrom.

In its chief sacrament, the official Christian Church perpetuates, after one manner or another, a rite or office whereby, it is taught, supernatural sustenance is communicated to the human soul. But if the doctrine affirmed in most schools of religious philosophy be correct—namely, that which is below is in correspondence with that which is above, and that visible things are patterns of invisible, it follows that the terrestrial office is a shadow of a celestial one; that the Church militant upon earth is the reflection of a Church triumphant beyond this earth, and that the sacramental bread and wine of the former have their appropriate, exalted, and sublimated counterparts in the latter.

Suppose it, then, possible for human consciousness to transcend terrestrial shadow-shapes, however sacred; to soar beyond the sacramental symbols inevitable to the perishable plane of existence, and to participate in the imperishable reality which, out of normal ken, stands behind the symbol and renders that symbol both possible and valid! Well, so to do would be to gain access to an interior Church hidden from this world and to partake of the arch-natural Eucharist therein celebrated. In other words, it would be to achieve that quest of the Holy Graal, to which, as its goal and *summum botiutn*, the knighthood of *religio*-romance literature was self-dedicated. That knighthood no wise abjured or neglected the instituted temporal rite of which we all know something. Rather did it strive to penetrate beyond the sacramental symbol and to find that symbol's legitimate and natural, or rather arch-natural, extension upon the spiritual plane. The symbol held good *pro tanto* **(for more)**; it was the conduit, the promise, and the substitution in time and space of a vital reality existent beyond those limitations; it was the base from which the questing knights operated and advanced. They dared not neglect the formal rite, but they ever realized that—

> *"A substitute shines brightly as a king*
> *Until the king be by; and then his state.*
> *Empties itself, as doth an inland brook*
> *Into the main of waters";*

and the objective of their quest was the transcending of symbol and substitute by attaining conscious cognition of the King—of kings—Himself.

Listen to the simple, stately prose of Malory describing Galahad's achievement of the Graal in Castle Corbenic:

"It seemed then that there came a man and four angels from heaven, clothed in the likeness of bishops, and had a cross in his hand; and the four angels bear him up in a chair, and set him down before the table of silver where the Sancgreal was; and it seemed that he had in the midst of his forehead letters that said, 'See ye here, Joseph, the first bishop of Christendom, the same which our Lord succored in Sarras, in the spiritual place.' . . . And then the bishop made semblance as though he would have gone to the consecrating of the mass, and then he took a wafer, which was made in the likeness of bread; and at the lifting up there came a figure in the likeness of a child, and the visage was as red and as bright as any fire, and smote himself into that bread, so that they all saw the bread was formed of a fleshy man. And then he put it into the holy vessel again and then he did that belonged unto a priest to do at mass. . . . Then looked they and saw a man come out of the holy vessel, that had all the signs of the passion of Jesus Christ, bleeding all openly, and said, '*My knights, and my servants, and my true children, which be come out*' of deadly life, I will now no longer hide me from you, but ye shall see now a part of my secret and of my hidings. Now hold and receive the high meat which ye have so much desired."

It seems a far cry from these high mysteries to the body ecclesiastic we know; to its record of heresies and schisms; its conflicts concerning Transubstantiation and the Real Presence. But to recognize this fact is essential to the point to which I am leading up. Centuries ago Galahad achieved the quest, but, it is recorded, "since then was there never no man so hardy for to say that he had seen the Sangreal." It, and what it connotes, owing to human imperfection, was withdrawn into concealment. The inner Church passed out of men's thought and consciousness, leaving the terrestrial Church desolate and in widowhood, practicing maimed and impoverished rites; a cloud, as it were, resting upon the sanctuary. Yet, the legends run, there was given a large promise of the restoration of the Graal; and of the re-manifesting upon a larger scale than aforetime of all that was removed into hiddenness. And through the long years of inhibition and withdrawal the hidden Church has continued its work in silence but in real activity, whereof abundant tokens exist for those who have an eye for them. Finding no response in its external counterpart it has made its voice heard unmistakably elsewhere, not in its old-time tones, but in varying and feigned terms, if haply some few, hearing, might discern or be brought to the understanding of the withdrawn mysteries; terms of subterfuge and allegory; terms of Alchemy, of Kabbalism, of Rosicrucianism, of Masonry, of Templarism, of sundry secret schools; yet terms proclaiming, beneath whatsoever veils, always the same message, urging ever the same doctrine; the doctrine, that of the possibility of human regeneration; the message, that in due time the King will return to that Kingdom within us which we affirm in every *Paternoster* to be His.

So much may be premised by way of introduction to what is perhaps the most important and effective treatise upon Christian mysticism as yet published. Hitherto the Graal legends and romances have been the province, well-nigh exclusively, of students of folklore and mediaeval letters, who have found in them only such worth as their special equipment enabled them to perceive. Even for them, when all has been said, there has remained over (as in the faint recognition of the idea of a Graal Church existing concurrently with but interiorly to the official Church of the day) a certain surplus age of refractory material, irresolvable because out of affinity with that which canons of folklore and scholarship are adapted to treat. But it is just this excess which, as Mr. Waite points out, belongs to, and is explicable only by, the mystic. And it is this which gives students of the varieties of mystical religious expression the due to the facts that the Graal literature is one of concealed intention; that it is the ashes, as it were, of a great fire; the records of a great religious experience; the reminiscences of a school of initiation into those mysteries the existence of which in Christian times has been, and still is, as veritable a fact as the old-time mysteries of Egypt, of Chaldea, and of Greece. "It is only in its mystic sense that the Graal literature can repay study," Mr. Waite asserts. His book, accordingly, is addressed exclusively to, and is intelligible only by, readers of mystical tendencies. From the standpoint of mysticism alone, therefore, it is best to speak of it here, though, to the credit of its author's own abundant erudition, it must be recorded that, to justify his conclusions, he has skillfully collated and coordinated that literature, and at one stride has both met official scholarship upon its own ground and altogether surpassed its achievements by virtue of having applied to the subject his own special gifts and appropriate equipment. Quite probably the customary reproach will be urged at him that the mystic has read into his subject more than was ever there or intended to be there. One might as ineptly complain at Ruskin for deducing ethics from the dust of the earth; or at Wordsworth for seeing more in a primrose than did Peter Bell. The most commercially minded may recall that even upon the material plane, fortunes have been made by discerning eyes that have seen the potential value of waste products or that have detected diamonds or gold nuggets where others saw but day-mire or river-gravel. Is the exercise of the like faculty to be denied the religious mystic who, recognizing the marks and signs-manual of fellow-mystics who have trodden the path that leads from natural to supernatural life before him, is able out of his own knowledge to interpret them, and out of his own experience to vouch for their veracity? The objection referred to notwithstanding, henceforth all consideration of the Graal literature, whether of that known or of that yet untraced, is destined to be subjected to the criterion of Mr. Waite's interpretation; and, to dismiss the merely academic aspect of the subject, it may be asserted confidently that future scholarship will confirm rather than discredit the deductions he has reached. If the large and often conflicting Graal literature be, as Mr. Waite suggests, a progress from chaos towards order; a series, that is, of graduated efforts on the part of an old-world age to express, in terms of chivalry, the perennial problem, and to disclose the perpetual secret, of individual reintegration into that primal sanity humanity enjoyed before the Fall into matter,—efforts culminating in the record of the attainment of the Graal by Galahad, the perfected spiritual aspirant,—so, after a like manner, the extensive, but inconclusive, modem interrogation of that literature may be said to culminate here in this exhaustive and convincing volume by the most appropriately equipped of literary knights.

Mr. Waite has given us, however, not merely an exposition of the meaning and purpose of the Graal literature. His work is a guidebook to a variety of other mystical systems that since the outward Church became desolated have sprung up, have perpetuated in other forms a cognate doctrine, and have left behind them traces of their affiliation to that unmanifested center which is none other than the Hidden Church of the Holy Graal. Casual inquirers into the perplexing literature of Alchemy have long desired some simple statement of what all that strange commixture of religion and chemistry really means.

The equally monstrous unintelligibilities of Hermeticism and Kabbalism; the doubtful value, historical and otherwise, of semi-secret schools of symbolic doctrine such as Masonry—all systems apparently foreign to, and yet not subversive of, orthodox doctrine and official religious institutions—have long needed justifying, interpreting, and coordinating. Mr. Waite has supplied this need, and has furnished us with a common denominator to them all. He establishes beyond controversy the fact that they are all voices crying in the wilderness, in different tones, but expressive of all of one truth, and testifying all to a common but concealed source of inspiration.

Is there now for the plain wayfaring man who is unable or unwilling to tread these devious paths of apparent heterodoxy any instructional method ready to hand whereby he may enter upon the heritage promised by them all? Can he, not being a knight-errant, behold the Graal today? Can he, no alchemist, transmute base metals into gold; or, no builder of temples, discover a certain lost secret, by which he may rear one? Well, in each of these cases, the goal is the same, and all the various methods of attainment are reducible to one; that one, as Mr. Waite succeeds in demonstrating, being involved in the true perception of the Catholic office of the Mass; an office which, in whatever other respects, the Latin Church may have deflected from its purpose, it yet, by an unerring instinct, has perpetuated and preserved from desecration as a channel of supernatural grace and a criterion for universal guidance. It is perhaps a strange claim to be made by one outside that Church and to readers, many of whom will be prejudiced against its communion. But Mr. Waite's claim is not used at all as an argument for enlistment in the Roman Church. He knows too well that the offices of grace are administered upon all hands and are not restricted to any one ecclesiastical penfold. As an expert, if the term be permitted, in mysticism and symbolism, he merely records and emphasizes, with equal sincerity and impartiality, the fact that, despite all withdrawals of the hallows, despite all spiritual blindness in official places, one eloquent witness to a supernal sacrament has always survived, and that all other symbolic and mystical systems find their simplest and readiest expression in the Roman Office of the Mass. As in a great cathedral are found lesser shrines devoted to special purposes, and chapels subsidiary to the main sanctuary, so Mr. Waite's thesis is designed to show that all mystical schools and systems outside the main current of historic orthodoxy have in reality been but accessory to it; specialized forms appropriate at certain eras and to certain minds; yet all over-spanned by one common, embracing roof, and all capable of finding their diversified methods of expression unified at one central high altar. The alchemic mystery, for example, as Mr. Waite proves, is put with almost naked simplicity in Eucharistic doctrine. To understand the Mass is to hold the key to all other mystical systems.

I have left small space for reference to Mr. Waite's most important and instructive pronouncement upon the nature of that Hidden Church, which, never slumbering nor sleeping, has through the centuries of inhibition, watched over all the external churches and schools. Something of this unmanifested communion of saints we have learned before from those enlightening letters of Eckhartshausen's in The Cloud upon the Sanctuary, and from other less well-known sources. Henceforth, all such voices will find fuller and coordinated expression in Mr. Waite's earnest and impressive closing pages. He defines it variously as the integration of sanctified souls in the higher consciousness; the cohort of just men made perfect; the lower mind of the official Churches raised to a higher plane of self-realization and rendered conscious of the unmanifested life involved within itself. It is not an organized community in time and space, and yet life within physical limitations need be no disqualification for admission thereinto. It is briefly that hidden House into which, in the passage quoted above, the purified spirit of man, typified by Galahad, is described as entering and participating in the celebration of the supreme mysteries of being; that House into which, as the Graal romances tell, and as our experience attests, the hallows have for a season been withdrawn, leaving a widowed Church with but their substitution, though not without promise of their restoration. Is Mr. Waite's book—as I have said, the most luminous and important work upon Christian mysticism yet given us—a presage that the restoration is impending? That is a question that will be answered affirmatively or negatively according to the measure of enlightenment and mystical consciousness of him to whom it is put. Assuredly no one will read this book without asking it of himself, and without wondering why, at the present juncture in human affairs, when the questing spirit for the things of final import is rife amongst us, so momentous an elucidation of matters that for so long have remained veiled and close-guarded should have taken place. And no understanding reader will close it without gratitude and without praying that it may fulfil its author's purpose of helping many upon the path of attainment of that of which his book treats.

Walter L. Wilmshurst

THE MYSTICAL IDEAL AS EXPRESSED IN POETRY

WHEN mysticism speaks, it speaks in music; the two terms are essentially, as they are etymologically, related. For mystical utterance is the voice of purified emotion; it is the soul, speaking, as nearly as its physical limitations permit, after a spiritual manner. All other speech, the issue of the mind rather than of the soul, is relatively mere mouthing, and as though mind and reason must needs be employed to ensure intelligibility and regulate the expression and form of what the soul seeks to express, yet the value of the expression is proportional to its freedom from the warping, clouding influences of ratiocination and the deflective action of intellectual prejudice. Silence we know to be often the best speech, since the greatest things surpass expression; but since humanity, like Nature, is impelled to give expression even to silence and to things which silence would best express, the fact stands that the purest and truest of vocal utterances come *ex ore infantium* **(out of the mouth of babes)**—out of the mouth of babes, of whatever age in point of mortal years, but young and fresh in spirit, whether children, seers or poets.

> *Thou Primal Love, that gran test wings*
> *And voices unto woodland birds.*
> *Grant me the gift of saying things*
> *Too simple and too sweet for words!*

In this quatrain from The Angel in the House, verbally and emotionally so exquisitely simple, yet imaginatively so comprehensive and exalted, one hears as it were the naïve voice of aboriginal, unsophisticated man, but recently *ex-paradised*, striving to sing the songs of his spirit in a strange land, yet hampered by an inadequate organ of expression and envious of that of orders of life less noble than himself but possessing one commensurate with their ordained status.

The logical reason speaks in prose, and prosaically; the native voice of the soul, like that of the world-soul, is rhythmic, poetical, mystical, and the truest poetry is that of the truest mystic. Poetry is the quest of the Beauty lying beneath the surface of any given subject-matter. But what is that Beauty? It is itself something mystical, unanalyzable; not one but an aggregate of pleasing qualities; an assemblage of perfections brought to a focus; a confluence and synthesis of virtues natural and ultra-natural. Plato, in the Phaedrus, anticipating by six centuries the very words of the Christian gospel, affirmed that absolute Beauty, of which all glints of terrene beauty are but iridescent reflexes, exists objectively upon a transcendental plane of life, "shining in company with the celestial forms," and that a man initiated into a direct cognition of It will leave all, father and mother, brethren and companions, and despise loss and contumely, to follow It and sleep by its side as a servant. The ideal of the Hebrew prophet was to "see the King in His beauty." Keats epitomized philosophy in the phrase:

Beauty is Truth; Truth, Beauty; this is all
Ye know on earth, and all ye need to know.

It is the subject of two of the noble *Fowre Hymmes* of Spenser. It is the theme of that truest of nursery-myths which tells of a Sleeping Beauty long drowsing in a tangled forest and awaiting but the reviving kiss of a lover bold enough to win a way through to her. But this is but a variant of other cosmic parables telling of a Lost Word waiting to be found; of a ruined Temple needing to be rebuilt; of a removed Graal; of kings and ideal men sore wounded and departed towards the sunset; all legends of man's fall and loss; parables of his present dream-life amid illusions, until an awakening kiss comes and restores, or sets him upon the path to, his primal rights.

There is no source from which the kiss may not come, for all things conspire to minister to man's awakening. Wordsworth received it in the vocal solitudes of virginal nature, and was caught up out of the sense-world to a recollection of the superb glory of an antecedent life and of "that imperial palace whence he came." But he discerned that the glory was nowise banished even here; but shrouded and occulted rather as by some Merlin-magic; ever ready to "flash upon the inward eye" receptive to its impressions, and ever exercising a beneficent, formative influence upon human life; cloud and tree, storm and star, mountain and rivulet, each contributing its subtle ministry towards man's reintegration and causing "beauty born of murmuring sound," to pass into his face.

To Coventry Patmore, the appeal of the ideal Beauty beckoned through the faces of women.

Her beauty was a godly grace;
The mystery of loveliness
Which made an altar of her face
Was not of the flesh, though that was fair,
But a most pure and living light
Without a name, by which the rare
And virtuous spirit flamed to sight;

and this vision of the "veiled virgin" led him on to the deeper truth of the profound sacramentalism of inter-sexual attraction; a phenomenon predicative of the ultimate marriage in consciousness of affinitized souls, and further, of these, when so wedded, with the Divine Soul, which is restless until its segregated rays coalesce in their original unity. He saw the divine in man seeking union, beneath all physical folds and beyond all sensual taint, with the divine in woman, and a prophetic outburst in his *Sponsa Dei*, at a stroke, discloses the fallacy of human separateness, emphasizes the fundamental but as yet unrealized unity of life, and reveals the truth that every inter-flash of love between men and women is a shadow of what, in a fine paradox, he calls "The love that is *between Himself*."

> *Oh, Heart, remember thee That man is none Save one.*
> *What if this lady be thy soul, and he*
> *Who claims to enjoy her sacred beauty be*
> *Not thou, but God; and thy sick fire*
> *A reflex heat Flash'd on thy cheek from*
> *His immense desire*
> *Which waits to crown, beyond thy brain's conceit,*
> *Thy nameless, secret, hopeless longing sweet.*
> *Not by and by, but now?*

And to some, the initiation comes not from natural sources but through the doctrine and artificial offices of instituted religion. Of such was Francis Thompson, one of the very greatest of mystical poets, who upon the Thames Embankment spent abject and penurious nights that yet rewarded him with the sight of the Beatific Vision "pitched between Heaven and Charing Cross." A son of the Roman Church, it fell to him, as Patmore recorded, to exploit "the inexhaustible and well-nigh wholly unworked mine of catholic philosophy." To him, the universe showed as one vast sanctuary wherein a "Titanian primal liturgy," of which the temporal reflex is that of the Church, is sung perpetually; the sun an officiating priest, the earth itself a censer slowly being swung by some mighty spirit unknown in adoration before an unseen high altar. His gorgeous verse is perhaps the greatest justification extant in poetry of the doctrines of renunciation and the cross, by means of which he reconciled the conflicting opposites of the world's pain and joy, and unified ideal Beauty with all that seems at first to negate it and to prevent its manifesting. To his cleansed vision that latent Beauty was everywhere present: it might be seen by us all if we looked, as Wm. Blake used to say, "not with but through the eye" of the senses.

The angels keep their ancient places;
Turn but a stone, and start a wing!
'Tis ye; 'tis your estranged faces
That miss the many-splendoured thing.

Only the splendor of his work and the richness and imminence of his accorded vision, one feels, can justify the price exacted for it in his own life-tragedy. "There goes the man who has been in hell," people whispered as Dante passed; and, to use Thompson's own words, to

Drink the moonless mere of sighs
And tread the places infamous to tell
Where God wipes not the tears from any eyes,
Where through the paths of dreadful greatness are,

seems, as the common history of the greater mystics testifies, to be a prerequisite to the great awakening.

The foregoing sketch of types of mystical poetry, inspired from different sources but disclosing a common term, is intended to prelude a notice of the poetical works of Mr. A. E. Waite. These stand, and that prominently, in the direct line of succession of highly illuminated utterance. A purely literary appraisement might adjudge his verse, as such merely, below the supreme level of attainment which has secured for the great names already mentioned canonization among the classics. Yet it is always admirable never otherwise than chaste, ardent and sincere, and lacking perhaps in no other merely literary merit than the power to coin frequent striking phrases—*aurea dicta* that "twinkle like Sirius on a frosty night," haunting the memory and compelling quotation; a capacity, by the way, which the author displays abundantly when employing the medium of prose. But from the mystical standpoint, one has no reservation to make; the purely literary deficiency (though I fear that this word is much too strong) is atoned for by the range and grandeur and many-sidedness of his conceptions. With many poets, the moments of authentic inspiration are few. The flame leaps from the altar to touch the heights for an instant, and then relapses to a modest glow; or perhaps some aspect of truth is offered tentatively or apologetically; or in a moment of exaltation, some precious glimpse is captured which is truer for the reader than for the instrument who gives it lyrical expression. But Mr. Waite's message is not sporadic, but systematic. He writes always with and from the open vision, and with his feet upon the rock of knowledge and tested, first-hand, spiritual experience. His voice is that of one who has climbed to certain heights above his laboring fellows and shouts down to them an assurance that the path upwards is safe and sure, if severe, and that beyond the wreathing clouds he has seen peaks that will well repay the climb. He is expositor and encourager as well as seer and poet.

There are things of which it has been said, as of that Sleeping Beauty before-mentioned, that the outward eye hath not seen nor ear heard; yet those who have said such things must, by the hypothesis, have entered, as Mr. Waite gives evidence of having done, into conscious relations with them by another process than that of the senses. Heart-hunger to attain to this process is common to us all; but the fact that the hunger exists is also the earnest that the travail of our hearts shall be satisfied, a matter upon which Mr. Waite gives full assurance in some tender, winning verses entitled A Confidence:

That which you seek for in your heart of hearts, That which transcends both Nature and the Arts, Great beyond conscious grasp of human mind. But ever as the rest and goal Acknowledged by your secret soul,—Brother, I promise, you shall surely find.

And if you ask me—knowing it so great—The solid ground on which I dare to state That you shall certainly attain at length; Learn that beyond the things which seem I have divined your dream. And also know your hidden source of strength.

Have courage, therefore: Keep your daily road, And after your own individual mode Do that which comes to hand, but well and true; For failures sometimes made—as such—Be, not concern'd too much. Fear not yourself;—I have no fear for you.

And if you wish to know further as to the supreme secret, you will find it here written—by way of restating an ancient doctrine that tells of a passport that "never faileth,"—that the secret is one for those Whose souls are subtly link'd with things above By sanctified capacities of love. . . . Know too the work is love's, and love's the call, While love is also the material. And at the end such union comes at length As to the worker brings another strength Those heights forsaken once again to dare, Those realms discover which await him there; With consciousness of ends beyond them still,—The holy palace, the eternal hill;

And thus it comes about that with "the glorious company of the apostles" of poetry who have striven to express the mystical Ideal in verse, and from whose evangels have here been collated a few typical and mutually-corroborative testimonies, it may be claimed that Mr. Waite is to be numbered as one who speaks with a confidence, and perhaps with an experience, that is excelled by none, and with a variety of expression and form attained to by few.

Mr. Waite's philosophical base is the catholic thesis that human life is passing at the periphery of a circle whose center is our true and eventual home. And his one cry is, Who goes home?—home out of strange houses of sleep where the soul drowses under the myriad enchantments that make up what our dull senses persuade us into imagining is life. Nature herself (and here Mr. Waite expands Wordsworth's message) is ever crying to man, "Awake, thou that sleepest." Everything sub-human offers kisses sacramental of the great awakening one that is suprahuman, saying as it were, "I, too, sleep till you awake; I, too, suffer arrested ministry till you are made whole; till the Lost Word is found, till the King returns from the West, and the Graal is restored." Mr. Waite, who elsewhere has interpreted at length the import of these great legends of cosmic loss, brings before the mind with great art the sense of the spiritual Beauty and realities underlying the cortex of physical life and needing but the release of a dormant faculty to ensure their perception. In *The King's Rendering*, a superb poem, presaging things that shall be, he gives us the vision of the return of the mystic King from Avalon with the Graal; the invisible procession entering London from the west at dawn, and passing through the awakening life of the streets to restore the withdrawn hallows to the Minster altar, whilst the dull citizens are gradually startled from their spiritual lethargy by light kindling in the East and by the shouts of a ragged, homeless lad roused to vision and worship by the brushing against his naked leg of the robe of one in the passing cavalcade of angels. This is poetry at its noblest; but Mr. Waite's implication is that there remains something nobler still—namely, the personal realization of what this vision implies; and the gist of his meaning is lost unless one sees that the city the King must enter is within us; that the altar awaiting the Graal is the sanctuary of the individual soul, and that its restoration is a present possibility.

Nature herself, then, awaits the re-integration of that which is her center—namely, man. She is inarticulate, save for sacramental whispers, because he is; let him but speak the word of power and she, too, will be made whole. She is dependent upon him, and the apparent antagonism between him and her is due to her reaction against his neglect to recognize the fact. Here is a passage typical of Mr. Waite's great sweep of vision, embracing earth, man, and heaven simultaneously:

> *All thing on sea and land*
> *Speak to my soul, and each*
> *Blithe voice I understand*
> *Answers in flowing speech.*

Quantities, measures, rhymes,
Harp string and organ-note
Surround me at all times;
Stars that in ether float,
Sun in his flaming course,
All the world's lights and all
Darkness and tempest's force
Thrill me with frequent call.
Bear I no tidings true
Which all might hear and learn,
Plain Nature, simple view,
And little child discern?
Soul high-encompassed, tell!
Surely the world can know
How the small fonts as well
As great with mercy flow;
Grace to the humblest field of daily life is lent,
For each is sign'd and seal'd
With marks of sacrament.
In Wall Street dare we say
An office God disowns?
Why, angels pass that way
As by the Masters' thrones.
The keen winds sweeping there
Do proud hosannas sing.
Yea, even as in the fair
White City of the King.

From the sacramentalism of Nature, from that of the great myths and legends, from the coordination of all these in the instituted rites of official religion, Mr. Waite bids us come up still higher and behold the prototypes behind the sacramental phenomena; to assist in thought at the heavenly

Mass; to watch, the Holy Sacrifice ever being offered behind all veils; and to perceive the hidden mysteries perpetually operating to secure the return of man to the Center. Upon this side of his work, Mr. Waite's genius connects with Francis Thompson's. His *Poor Brother's Mass Book* is an esoteric and interpretative commentary graduated to the external incidents of the Eucharistic Office; a wonderful adjunct to the formal text of the missal, intended to lift the imagination above the bonds of the letter, and one that may serve to elevate the consciousness into places high above all sacramentalism. Such a consummation would surely be the crown of the ministry of poetry; and poetry is itself, for many, a most potent minister in revealing that Beauty which I have said to be the subject of all mystical quests and which all witnesses testify to be everywhere present, but to be sleeping. Exigencies of space, and the quasi-dramatic form of much of Mr. Waite's poetical work, prevent further quotation here, but perhaps enough has been said to send readers to his two volumes, sumptuous alike in form and content, at first hand. I will add only that Mr. Waite's poems earn a title to something more than the poet's conventional bays, and I would fain offer my own *obolus* of thanksgiving. His work carries with it a claim to that tribute, which is due to the servitors and illuminators of humanity; and although, such is the nature of the times, there may be few able to pay it, or who are even conscious of the obligation, there are grounds for believing that the wages do not go unpaid.

S. WINEFRIDE'S WELL AND LEGEND

I - The Well

S WINEFRIDE, most admirable Virgin, even in this unbelieving generation still miraculous, pray for us! In the small Flintshire town of Holywell, overlooking the "sands o' Dee" these words are made to haunt one. Our habitual mental focus is not readily readjusted, but a visit to the Well and Shrine of the seventh century Cambro-British saint urges one to make the effort. The conditions of our times are such that they compel most of us willy-nilly to bow down in the House of Rimmon, and matters that to our forebears seemed reasonable and credible enough assume for us a quite contrary appearance. Probably—and some of us at least believe the assumption justified—however much man's mental focus alters from age to age the object of full and perfect vision is static and varies not. The pupils of humanity's eyes may see for the moment, but a part of that object as through a glass darkly; may dilate with wonder, adoration and even, maybe, with credulity; or they may contract in criticism and denial, without affecting the totality of what lies waiting to be perceived. From a proverbial age of miracles we glide into one repudiating the possibility of miracle, and it comes about that to days that seem to us a monument of credulity ours would have seemed a corresponding miracle of unbelief. But since to talk thus is but to argue in a circle and to beg the whole slippery question as to what miracle involves, it seems safer to assert that each age is characterized by its own peculiar wonders, sees its own special visions, and is thereby self-blinded to those of other times; and he is wise who can adjust his own sight to shifting conditions and who can reconcile and synthesize in just perspective the varying perceptions of different periods.

Walter L. Wilmshurst

S. WINEFRIDE'S WELL, EXTERIOR ; ENTRANCE LODGE (BELOW) AND CHAPEL.

Holywell is situate two miles from its railway station, at the English end of the North Wales Riviera, and is reached by a road leading uphill through a broad ravine known locally as Sechnant, the dry valley, for before the waters from the wonderful well began to stream down it fourteen centuries ago it was, as the name "sech" implies, waterless and dry. At the head of the valley stands a sixteenth-century chapel or oratory, in the crypt of which is the famous well, and immediately adjoining is Trefynnon, "the settlement by the Well," or a notice Holywell, whence one may look down upon the broad estuary of the Dee just about to join the sea. The place has few attractions; the valley renders the air close and relaxing; material prosperity seems to have deserted it; some factories and one of the chief hotels are closed and derelict, whilst detached blocks and entire streets of small and often squalid cottages are conspicuous and bespeak by sundry tokens the presence of many Irish, much poverty, and that unprogressiveness in social and temporal matters which, to whatsoever cause attributable, is so often found associated with a poor and largely Roman Catholic populace. Amid these slums, however, are an admirably kept and appointed Catholic church and excellent schools, at the entrance to which stands a large, impressive figure of the Savior, beneath whose hands of welcome and blessing every child that enters must pass. It is well and to the honor of the Church whose foresight prescribes these things, that those whose lives are perforce spent in mean houses and cheerless conditions should be reminded, by the presence among them of such striking symbols, of unseen providences and of the promise of fair habitations and tabernacles not made with hands.

The Well is by the roadside and may be entered by a turnstile for two pence. Two pence more secures a towel and bathing dress if you propose to bathe. You reach first an uncovered oblong pool shaped like a modern swimming-bath, stone built, surrounded by dressing boxes, and some three feet deep. The water is entered by some steps, near the foot of which and immersed in the clear water is an aged, irregular slab of rock, known as S. Beuno's Stone, upon which, as a center of devotion, pilgrims are directed to kneel, and of which I shall say more presently. From this pool, an outer court of the Gentiles as it were, one passes into the inner sanctuary, which is the crypt of a chapel or oratory, once of great richness and beauty but now weather-worn and somewhat dilapidated, built upon the site of earlier premises shortly before the Reformation by Margaret Beaufort, mother of Henry VII, in association with various noble families, in the style of the well-known chapel bearing that King's name at Westminster Abbey. In the center of this crypt and surrounded by an ambulatory is a large hexagonal stone basin, some eight or ten feet deep, from the rocky floor of which wells, and has welled, it is said, for fourteen centuries, the miraculous spring of water, crystal clear, with a faint green tinge. Slowly, steadily, and with scarcely an indication of being in motion, the water surges up; *labitur et labetur in omne volubilis aevum* **(return and resume the stream flows)** at an even rate of 3,000 gallons per minute and at a mean temperature throughout the year of 540 F°. From this hexagonal basin the water overflows through an iron grille into a *piscina*, intended apparently as the chief, as doubtless it was the original, bathing-place—a narrow grave-shaped hollow in the ground and overlooked by a large crucifix. The size of this bath allows of but one bather entering at a time, who descends into it by stone steps and, after wading through, leaves it at the other end by like means. An altar-shrine and statue of S. Winefride stand close to this bath for the devotional purposes of pilgrims, and daily service is held here at noon. The water then flows from the grave-shaped *piscine* **(pool)** into the large oblong bath already mentioned, after which it passes away from consecrated premises to discharge secular offices. It first provides an adjoining brewery with machine-power, and presumably with the fluidic constituent of beer; renders a similar service to a flannel factory a little further on; and after forming the water-supply of the inhabitants of the valley, loses itself two miles away from its source in the broad Dee. The pillars and walls of the crypt covering the Well are festooned with candles, banners and votive offerings of crutches, splints, trusses, wreaths, written and even carved memorials contributed by grateful pilgrims who have benefited there. Many submerged stones of the Well show extensive stains or patches of rich red color. The mythopoeic tendencies of the ignorant in past ages have attributed these to the blood of S. Winefride, which, according to legend, was shed here and originated the Well, but modern critical scrutiny perceives them to be due to minute blood-colored mosses. It is fair to the ecclesiastical authorities in charge of the place to say that the latter explanation is the one accepted by them, as also that they recognize that the water of the Well yields to chemical analysis no properties whatever of a medicinal or specially curative nature.

Thing Pool; S. Beuno's Stone near steps on left. Crypt with small Bath and Spring beyond.

The spring is of ordinary water that has percolated down from the limestone uplands above Holywell and finds a vent in this valley, which forms its conduit to the Dec, the natural drainage system of the district. The large bath, I perceived, is not guiltless of the presence of sticklebacks; they are, however, innumerous, and for a pilgrim to catch sight of them is, I was told *pour rire*, a not unpropitious omen.

The fame of the Well today is, except perhaps among the Catholic community, at its nadir, largely doubtless in sympathy with the general indifference of the age towards almost any but commercial and secular interests; in part also owing to the greater celebrity of the modern Lourdes; and in some measure perhaps by reason of the contemptuous attitude towards it of the Protestant community in the district, certain of whom described it to me as "the Catholic fraud." It is patronized, however, especially in summer, by a steady attendance if not by a large number of visitors, the majority of whom seem to be of the poor Irish Catholic class from our great cities and industrial centers. I propose to say little here of cures effected at the Well. Records of numbers of such cases in both olden and modern times are to be found in the literature of the subject. In support of such claims in earlier times, the well must have had a considerable reputation as a healing center in the sixteenth century to justify the erection by people of distinction of the present buildings; whilst since that time numerous cures have been less or more well-authenticated and the cumulative testimony creates a strong presumption in favor of so-called "miracles" having occurred. Official bathing hours are appointed for each sex. Many pilgrims do not enter the water, but merely hold an arm or leg in it, bathe their faces or eyes, or drink of it; whilst many purchase specially provided cans to take water away for use in private or to dispatch to friends at a distance. It must be remembered that all who come are not physically afflicted; the visit may be made as an act of faith or devotion or to secure interior grace. To quote from the Pilgrims' Manual:

"Though most of the cures have been granted whilst bathing, it is by no means a necessary condition for obtaining signal favors and graces. Strong faith and persevering prayer are the first conditions. Many wonderful cures have been granted to those who have had a small quantity of the water sent to them at a distance. Others have been cured by external application of the water or of the relic of S. Winefride. No fixed rule can be given as to the number of baths. Many striking cures have been effected at a first bath; in other cases, the cure has not come till after three or nine or twenty or more baths have been taken. Further, three separate visits at intervals of a year or less are recommended by the tradition of the promise made by S. Beuno to S. Winefride that 'whoso ever shall three times implore thy aid in sickness or misfortune shall at least at the third time obtain his request, if it be not opposed to the Divine Will'. It is quite sufficient to pass three times through the little well and to kneel for a few seconds on S. Beuno's Stone."

Undeniable and outstanding features of the scene at the well are the poverty of most and the intense sincerity of all those who come in the quest for healing. There are cripples and blind, deformed and maimed, suffering adults of both sexes, and diseased infants but a few weeks old that one wishes had never been born. Many are here or are bringing their invalid friends or children here for whom no hope from medicine or surgery remains and who now, often after long periods of both physical and devotional preparation, have come in their trouble as to a last resource and in the hope that some signal favor may be vouchsafed towards their dire need. One sees pain of body and anxiety of mind concentrated here in an intensity sometimes almost maddening, were it not irradiated by the splendid courage and the sacred simplicity of faith that is manifest amid the cruel distress and the pitiable infirmity. I stand by the entrance-wicket, where literature, views, small images of saints, medals and sundry accessories are purchasable, to watch and listen. A woman comes for a quart tin of water to take away; another for a bit of weed or moss from the submerged stones of the well and supposed to possess healing properties—is not the weed "S. Winefride's hair?" The station omnibus draws up and discharges a medley freight of infirm devotees and their friends; one sees crutches and bandages, and discerns surgical appliances ill-concealed beneath the best clothes. "A statue of S. Anthony, please, and what time will do for Mrs. McNolan to be brought down to be taken into the water?" A decent, sad-looking working man comes up bearing a girl with head and arms hanging invertebrately as a rag doll over his shoulder. He has brought her from Lancashire and has no womenfolk to look after her; he could manage to pay for her stay here for a few weeks if someone would kindly take her in, but he must get back to his work to earn the needful money. It is a case for the nuns at the local hospice, and the poor, undersized child with wan face and frightened, dark glinting eyes—she looks five years old, I find she is eighteen—is taken to receive the care of the kind Sisters. (I saw her after her first bath; she had been carried through the water, after which she had already managed to stand up and was doing very nicely Amid this crowd of poor and infirm, luxury hoots up in its motor touring-car, pays its two pences to enter, spends ten minutes in looking round, asks a few questions, shrugs its shoulders at the replies, and hoots away again. (*S. Winefride . . . in this unbelieving generation . . pray for us*) Here is an aged, wizened dame with a crutch and obvious cataract, breathing wheezily as she hoists her old bones very slowly up the steps on her exit from the premises. She is assisted by a niece, a third of her age, whom she is scolding for cowardice in refusing to bathe and so preventing herself from doing. ("She's 94, and been to New Zealand six times," says the niece aside to me, "comes here every summer she can and says she'll go in the water tomorrow by herself if I won't go with her; she's that pluck!") A message comes for the attendant to carry through the bath some child or a poor wretch impotent to walk. A nurse in uniform enters with a little well-dressed boy who runs about the place quite happily and apparently in the best health; but round one of his bare knees is, alas! a stained bandage; it is a case of lupus. And here are three bright, hatless girls arm-in-arm, evidently holiday visitors from the seaside, chatting and laughing with a pleasantry almost unbecoming here; but no, the middle sister, I find, is totally blind. "The optic nerve has gone," they tell me, "and we understand what that means; so if anything happens here, we shall know there has been a miracle." Inside the large bath, there is considerable commotion. There is the splash of water and now and again the scream of a child or girl upon being taken into the cold pool. One lady is in great request, and is constantly in and out of the water and dressing or undressing. Presently I hear from her own lips that upon two separate occasions some years ago, she herself received her instantaneous relief that effected the elongation of a deformed leg in one case and in the other obviated amputation of the arm after an accident. As an act of thanksgiving, she comes now each summer to encourage and give confidence to other sufferers, and leading them into the water she recites for them the litany of S. Winefride and calls upon the bystanders to make the prescribed responses.

Upon another occasion, a refined, handsome lady comes to take one of a series of baths. There happens for the moment to be no other bathers present, and she enters the water alone. I retire for the time being from the bath, but the door chancing to be opened by an attendant I catch a brief and involuntary glimpse of her standing in the pool with closed eyes and lips moving in intensity of supplication, whilst with one hand she dashes water upon her hip. Later on in response to a complimentary remark made in my hearing upon her robust appearance, her ready and frank answer was:

Walter L. Wilmshurst

"Oh, there's nothing the matter with me. I come in the interests of others who cannot come themselves or have not the means to do so. I have a boy at home with hip-disease, for whose sake I bathe my own hip, and there are many others whose infirmities I come here each season to remember. It is not for me to say how or why cures result from my agency to people at a distance, but the fact remains that several of those in whose behalf I have come have benefited remarkably."

Undoubtedly cures take place, and Protestants and sceptics no less than Catholics have benefited from the well. Of course, there are many disappointments. Some cures are instantaneous, others occur gradually and after the patients have left the district for their homes. A few days before my recent visit a child of six, carried in a splint made to extend to every part of the body, had left the well whole after a single bath—the complicated surgical contrivance of steel and leather being left behind at S. Winefride's altar, where it now hangs as a memorial; a blind man had regained his sight; whilst a young woman who had arrived yesterday on crutches had been able to leave them behind after years of use, and I saw her gleefully but clumsily running about in her bathing dress after taking a further bath in the hope of completely curing her thin, distorted legs. To all inquiries made from those in official attendance at the well the sole answer elicited, and it is quite frank and sincere, is an allusion to the power of faith and the mysterious working of the Divine Will. Apart from all the religious or scientific questions involved, one cannot witness such scenes as these without considerable emotion. In a great hospital, one finds an even larger concentration of human wreckage and witnesses the grim business of surgery and medicine working in skilled, organized fashion to effect relief. Humanity in the health of body and the vigor of intellect is pitting itself to win as against humanity in pain and misery; there are recognized methods of procedure, rules of the game to be observed upon both sides to the struggle, and whilst the emotional aspect of the picture is not absent, the conditions which prevail prevent it from assuming emphasis, and it is neutralized by the predominating atmosphere of "business." But here things are different. The sense of tragedy is present; the pathos of it all is more poignant, and there are no conventions to restrain it. To those coming here, scientific skill has, as a rule said its last word, and that—one without hope. The demands made here are not those of the logical mind to the latest word of medical skill and to accredited methods of relief; they are cries to an ultimate unseen court of appeal, to potencies unknown and indeterminate; they are heart cries to something beyond the region of sense and logic; and far from appearing unworthy or unreasonable there is in them something of the quality of heroism from the fact that they are raised, and raised in confidence, in an age when the general tendency is towards stifling emotionalism and ridiculing all aspirations beyond the power of academic science to gratify. The purposes of a shrine of this nature are, I repeat, not restricted to physical healing alone, but since it is of physical relief that I speak for the moment, it must be recognized that in regard thereto two facts are patent; one, that the water of the well admittedly possesses no medicinal properties; the other, that cures, whether instantaneous, gradual, or of patients at a distance through the vicarious agency of their friends, are in fact effected. Wherein lies the explanation? Miracle, faith, autosuggestion, shock, psychic influences, or what not? But this question we will defer in order to approach it again after taking into consideration such light as may be gained from ascertaining, if it be so possible, the original purpose of the well.

So far from this Wellbeing, exceptional, sacred wells, wishing wells and curative bathing-places have existed throughout history. To water itself there has always been attributed profound symbolic significance, as the Hebrew and Christian Scriptures testify *passim*. "In water there is a quality endowed with a blessing," sings Taliesin, chief of the

Welsh Bards—contemporary, by the way, with S. Winefride—in a fine mystical poem in the *Mabinogion* that, telling in a parable the story of the human soul, its descent into the body of flesh and its redemption therefrom, relates how—

> *Into a dark leathern bag I was thrown*
> *And on a boundless sea I was sent adrift;*
> *Which was to me an omen of being tenderly nursed.*
> *And the Lord God then set me at liberty.*

But apart from any purposed religious attributions, running water has ever a subtle charm for us all. Our favorite recreation ground, like that of Shakespeare's Welshman, is—

> *By shallow rivers, by whose falls*
> *Melodious birds sing madrigals.*

Some deep, unanalyzed instinct leads us to the waterside—or is it the water itself that has some secret magnetic influence drawing us to it? However it be, the attraction is universal. The motive that draws the Hindu multitudes to bathe in the sacred Ganges manifests in our own Sankey-hymn choralists who look forward to the day when—

> *"We shall gather by the river," etc., etc.*

Oases in tropical deserts have a symbolic significance as well as a utilitarian purpose for their denizens. In pre-Christian Greece, Italy, Syria and Asia Minor springs of water, often associated with guardian genii or with the healing cultus of *Aesculapius* **(Greco-Roman god of medicine)**, were once abundant; Jacob's well, the rivers Abana and Pharpar, and the pool of Bethesda are among Biblical examples of them. And there is nothing surprising in the fact that the *religio*-romantic Celt should have reproduced so frequently as a phenomenon. To trace the true history of

Forgotten Essays

specific places is now impossible; origins are lost in the distant haze of folklore and primitive religion. The modem example of Lourdes seems to rest upon a footing of its own and, if we accept the authorized account of its genesis, to come within the category of discoveries which the author of the *Religio Medici* quaintly declares to be due to "the courteous revelations of spirits."

The official account of the origin of S. Winefride's Well is derived from two more or less mutually corroborative sources. The chief and longer was compiled in 1137 by Robert, Prior of Shrewsbury, who says he "collected it partly from detached writings preserved in churches of the district, and partly from the narratives of priests whose veracity is recommended by their venerable age and by the habit they wear." A shorter, perhaps rather earlier, version is by an unknown monk of Basingwerke, near Holywell. The well had been in use for 500 years before these authors' time—S. Winefride's life being attributed to the years 610-660—so that, although the well must have acquired great repute in the interval, the narratives are very considerably *à posteriori* and this at a date when literary records necessitate very critical scrutiny, however good the faith in which they were composed. The essential features of the legend are these:

Early in the seventh century a holy man, S. Beuno—well known in the annals of Welsh sanctity—wandered into Flintshire under divine guidance and was moved to apply to one Teuyth, the proprietor of three manors and father of but one child, a daughter named Brewi or Frewi, to ask for a grant of land upon which to build a chapel and say Mass to the advantage of the district. The request was granted and there was allotted to him the modem Holywell valley, then known as Sechnant, owing to its being waterless (Sech, *i.e.*, *siccus*; *sèche*; dry). He built a chapel, said his daily office, and undertook the education of the maid Brewi. One day her parents had gone to church, the girl remaining alone at home—in one version owing to sickness; in the other to prepare and bring to the church fire, water, salt and other things required for Mass. At this point Caradoc, the wild lawless son of a local chief, called at the house during a hunting expedition, asked for refreshment and to see the girl's father, but finding her alone made unwarranted overtures to her. Brewi, already dedicated to virginity and to the divine service, made a pretext to leave the room, and thereupon rushed from the house to gain protection in the chapel where the service was now proceeding. Caradoc followed and overtook her not far from the chapel, and upon her further resistance struck off her head with his sword, the head rolling down the ravine into the open door of the chapel. During the ensuing consternation, S. Beuno came down from the altar, lifted up the head, and recognizing its owner, uttered a curse upon the murderer and a prayer for the resuscitation of the girl. The former "melted away before their eyes, like wax before the fire," being swallowed up by a chasm in the earth, whilst as S. Beuno replaced the head upon its body, the girl returned to life and animation, showing only a slender white scar around her neck. At the place where her severed head had fallen, a great spring of water burst forth and has continued to flow from that day to this, thus forming the present holy well, whilst the stones stained by her blood have ever since been red-stained. Brewi thereafter was known by the new name of Gwen-frewi (*anglice*, Winifred); the prefix *Gwen* meaning white, in allusion to the whiteness of both her scar and her sanctity. After this ordeal she continued to remain under the spiritual guardianship of S. Beuno for some years, when he received a monition to go elsewhere. He, however, left her to carry on his and her own good work in the valley, and departing bestowed his blessing and three promises upon her; one, that the stones should never cease to show the red traces of her passion and be a memorial of her chastity; a second, that "whosoever shall at any time in whatever sorrow and suffering implore your aid for deliverance from sickness or misfortune, shall at the first, or the second, or certainly the third petition obtain his wish";

and a third, that when he had himself departed to "the habitation God will provide for me on the margin of the sea," a gift sent by her to him once a year should reach his hands. Now there chanced to be a rock projecting from the stream caused by the miraculous spring, upon which the good man had been wont to pray; it is the rock previously referred to as S. Beuno's Stone, and the legend concludes with the assertion that during the rest of her life Winefride each year made a cloak as a gift for S. Beuno; that on the vigil of St. John Baptist, she placed it upon the stone; that it was washed down the little stream into the big river—the Dee—and the big river carried it to the sea, whose waves bore it safely to the Saint. He appears to have taken up his new abode at Cynnog, on the Carnarvonshire peninsula, where the remains of his monastery still exist, and where unwetted by the water the cloak is said to have been washed up at his feet the following morning with unfailing regularity.

Now, read literally, here is an utterly impossible story. (*S. Winefride . . . in this unbelieving generation . . pray for us*) Some concession is at once afforded us by a statement in the officially issued "Life" that "no Catholic is bound to accept in its entirety the account as thus handed down to us . . . the details of the history have to rest on their own evidence . . . they were included in the old Sarum office but are not embodied in our present breviary"; for which relief much thanks I But before offering an interpretation which, by ascertaining the true and inward spirit of the legend, may preserve its truth after another than a literal manner, a preliminary clearing of the ground may be effected by reference to a few noteworthy points. The legend appears to be a composite, one containing elements deriving from Latin and Celtic religious sources, respectively. To Latin sources is probably due so much of the story as refers to (1) the father of Winefride, who owned three estates, and dedicated one of these along with his daughter to the divine service; the same legend obtains of the father of the Virgin Mary, as may be found in a sermon upon Our Lady by Tauler, the great friar preacher of Strasburg of the fourteenth century; (2) the martyrdom: which is seldom found in connection with Celtic saints; (3) the incident of the spring of water originating where Winefride's severed head struck the ground. As to this, the Bollandist Father de Smedt, S. J., who has collated the records, deposes to having met with no less than twelve occurrences of this kind in the lives of Cambro-British Saints, a fact which, whilst tending strongly to negative the historicity of such incidents, creates, nevertheless, by its very repetition and emphasis, an equally strong presumption in favor of the story of the death and resuscitation having been introduced with an ulterior purpose, and that of a figurative and mystical nature. Probably all these twelve occurrences are referable to a like tradition regarding S. Paul, which alleges that at his execution outside the walls of Rome, his head fell and bounded thrice upon the ground, whence three springs of water at once issued; the site, formerly known as *Aquae Salviae*—the Waters of Salvation—is now called Tre Fontane (*Tres Fontes*), a name suspiciously like Trefynnon, the Welsh name for Holywell. (4) The incident of the liquefaction and disappearance of the murderer, also of Latin origin, corresponds with several similar occurrences to redoubtable sinners who had the misfortune to fall foul of this or that Welsh saint. It may be regarded as purely symbolical of the annihilation of evil by goodness.

But the final part of the legend, concerning Winefride's yearly gift to S. Beuno, of its deposit upon the stone and its unwetted transportation to his dwelling-place, has not a Latin but a strong Celtic savor. Again, we must not read literally; so to do involves obvious incredibility's. Moreover, a similar incident occurs in the life of the Irish S. Lenanus, whilst in Celtic hagiology frequent tales are to be found of tokens and of holy men drifting in rudderless boats over the waters to providentially appointed places. It remains, then, to see if it be possible to determine with any degree of probability as to its truth what idea, if any, underlies an episode of this character and why it should have been made the appendage and anticlimax of the central dramatic incident of the reputed minder and reanimation of S. Winefride, which in turn, as already suggested, may be merely a veil covering some interior intention.

Now where primary evidence is, as here, inaccessible, any hypothesis offered can be but an effort of the imagination and its plausibility is supportable only by reference to well-recognized methods of symbolical imagery employed elsewhere for the dual purpose of veiling and expressing religious truths. The present legend is full of suggestiveness, as also of affinities with other legends, and it is difficult to account for the invention of so elaborate a story and for its long and tenacious perpetuation save upon the supposition that originally it possessed a basis of truth of some kind, and not necessarily of a historical or objective nature. To the nebulous ages before that of modem letters is attributable to a vast quantity of folklore, myths, fairy-tales and romances, some of which still survive, embodying, as, *e.g.*, the Graal legends, in often extremely subtle and beautiful ways, profound religious and philosophical truths, though seldom recognized nowadays as enshrining such. Owing to its affinity with analogous coeval legends and to its own internal evidence, there are, I think, warrants for supposing the Winefride story to be of this nature. In origin it may have been that the legend was compiled, whether with or without reference to any actual historic person or event, as one purposely fabricated in *quasi*-historical form, but without intent that it should be treated as history; that it was a parable intended for use in connection with some simple religious rite in times before the Roman supplanted the Celtic Church and for the offices of the former substituted its own. Those familiar with the *quasi*-historic legend of the mythical Hebrew Hiram Abiff and with the purpose to which it has been applied will be best able to follow my suggestion that the legend of S. Winefride may once have served a similar purpose; a purpose that became abrogated upon the introduction of the sacramental offices, especially that of baptism, of the Latin church (which, however, undoubtedly took over the well and permitted the continuance of the legend in an adapted and elaborated form) and that in process of time became lost sight of utterly. There is, I am told, in Pembrokeshire, another holy well of little modern repute, the water of which is traditionally served by a hereditary custodian in the skull of a saint. Now, if this simple rite ever had any symbolic religious significance, which is probable, it implies that the water, which "springs up unto everlasting life", is attainable only by the path of sanctity and self-mortification. And it is hence no far cry from this well to that of S. Winefride, where it is still the duty of the pilgrim seeking health or grace to walk thrice through the waters filling a symbolic grave. As said above, the small and chief bath is a grave-shaped excavation, and though of sixteenth century construction, this *sepulchral piscina* doubtless is a faithful reproduction of one that for many centuries had anteceded it.

Whatever else may be said for it, the legend of S. Winefride is surely a parable of the soul's life; one of the many parables and figures by which religious truth was taught in early unlettered days. Under the familiar image of a chaste woman the virginal soul is depicted as yielding itself to the claims of its own higher and better part personified by the wandering Beuno, who "hath not where to lay his head" until someone grants him a place of rest where he can build a "church," Teuyth's three manors being a figure for the three estates of the human realm: body, soul, and spirit. There ensues a period of self-dedication and discipline in anticipation of the great regenerative change, and of this the imagery lies in Winefride's years of education by the saint and in her being actually engaged in preparing the elements for the Holy Sacrifice—the symbol of her own passion—at the very moment that the dark powers in the guise of the lustful Caradoc enter and make trial of her. It is noteworthy that the place of her preparation and trial is Sech-nant, the dry valley, for the soul's quest occurs in the wilderness of this world and in conditions of inward aridity; and this again connects with the Psalmist's "valley of the shadow of death" and with Ezekiel's "valley of dry bones." Her decapitation and subsequent resuscitation, coupled with the extinction of the evil power, are but a portrayal of what in the annals of sanctity of all faiths are known as mystical death and its inevitable consequent, mystical rebirth. After this she is given the "new name" that in Christian doctrine distinguishes the regenerate from the unregenerated man. That around a voluble and notable spring of water a legend of this nature should have been compiled by old-time religious instructors with a keen eye for the sacramentalism of natural phenomena, such as the bards possessed, and with a view to the spiritual edification of a semi-barbarous people is, I submit, entirely probable. It is impossible in the absence of positive evidence to put the claim higher than this or to disprove it, and the suggestion is here offered for what it may be worth.

We come now to that other part of the legend concerning S. Beuno's stone and to his removal, when his transmutative work in the Dry Valley was done, to an unknown, divinely-appointed place where at the sanctified Winefride, or that which she personifies, could communicate with him supernaturally. The stone immersed in the well, upon which pilgrims still kneel in emulation of S. Beuno, who so used it, suggests a connection with many other sacred stones, all having a common symbolic value and root. The Kaabeh adored at Mecca is for the Moslem pilgrim the symbol of the basal Reality which underlies all manifested things and "without which there is nothing made that is made." The reputed stone of Jacob in the Coronation-chair at Westminster is another emblem of that strength from and to which all other power must needs emanate and be referable; of that rock "upon which," it is recorded, "I will build my Church," and to which S. Paul alludes in saying, "And that rock was Christ." Again, those acquainted with the symbolical terminology of the spiritual alchemists will recall the philosophical "stone" which is to be found in the philosophical "water that wetteth not the hands," just as the cloak dispatched by Winefride reached S. Beuno undamped, and though it were vain to suggest that the Hermetic tradition, as such, was known in Wales in the seventh century, the fact remains that an equivalent idea or doctrine has persisted through the ages and has been reproduced in various ways. In virtue of this symbolism, the traditional devotion upon S. Beuno's immersed stone by pilgrims assumes the nature of an extremely appropriate and sacramental act of faith, and this in a degree far greater than is perhaps recognized by those who perform it, owing to the story's concealed significance having become lost.

There remains that romantic and extremely beautiful episode of S. Winefride's cloak yearly deposited on the stone and transmitted thence by water to S. Beuno at his distant and unknown home. Here, it may be, is concealed a reference to a very high doctrine; to that, namely, of the Communion of Saints; the interfusion of consciousness in a Holy Assembly of souls that have attained to an exalted, perfected state possible only to the sanctified. Again, I refrain from being dogmatic, but I confess to a personal intuition that tells me that in this incident there is both the promise and the echo of a fulfilment of that benediction of the Church which says *Ad societatem civium supernorum per ducat nos Rex Angelorum!* **(King leads us to the high realm of angels)** Readers familiar with two great books upon this subject, Eckartshausen's *Cloud upon the Sanctuary* and Mr. Waite's *Hidden Church of the Holy Graal* will follow my meaning and know the Christian aspect of this high theme. But so universal is the symbolic imagery of cloaks and wedding-garments, of streaming water, and of the great sea, that I suppose an enlightened Buddhist or Vedantist would readily apprehend the sense of this marvelous piece of Celtic mysticism, and would discern in the cloak an allusion to a subtler vehicle of consciousness than the physical organism, a vehicle by which it is possible for the higher mentality of man to transcend the normal brain states and, as "the dewdrop slips into the shining sea," to pass into that "conscious rest in omniscience" which in the orient is called Nirvana and in the Christian fold the Divine Union. The contemptuous Welsh Nonconformist spoke to me of S. Winefride's Well and its associations as "the Catholic fraud." I dare say that sometimes at the conventicle of his dismal sect he joins in singing, not, I hope, without interior relish, a gracious and well-worn hymn in which are the words—

Till in the ocean of Thy love
We lose ourselves in heaven above.

If so, he little suspects his unconscious testification to what is involved in the story of Winefride's "cloak" journeying over the waves "to a habitation by the sea, appointed by God." The suggestion here offered, then, is that S. Winefride's Well was once a center of Celtic Christianity where religious instruction was imparted through the medium of a primitive legend, and that both the well and the legend in an elaborated form were assumed and taken over subsequently by the Roman Church. That the inner purport of the imparted doctrine, intended primarily to be of a mystical nature, should in process of time have become lost, and the well reduced from its first intention to a place of pilgrimage for, almost exclusively, the cure of bodily disease, is only to say that they have shared the general process of materialization which every expression of spiritual truth sooner or later undergoes in the public mind. One need not, however, conclude that bodily cures were excluded from the original intention of the place, for physical health has often a direct connection with interior wellbeing. The power that can heal and uplift that part of our organisms which is higher than the physical has *a fortiori* at least equal jurisdiction over our grosser part, and the body is redeemable no less than the soul. Indeed, we are coming nowadays to discern the mutual interdependence of the two; to recognize that there is a sense in which the twain are one or may become at one; that even the material husk of ourselves and of all else is in its nature psychical; and that action and reaction are, for good or evil, continually passing between the multifarious constituents of that great pan-psychic Unity which we call the World. And herein—apart from all ultra-human potencies and possibilities, as to which it is not my business here to speak—lies a clue to the problem of the healings that are spoken of as "miraculous." The psychic forces generated in a shrine like this by the intense yearnings, the faith, and the aspirations of the troops of our afflicted brethren who for fourteen centuries have been visiting it in quest of life and healing, are not, be assured, utterly lost or wasted energies. The atmosphere of the place is charged with them. They have penetrated its walls and have soaked into its ancient stones until the accumulated force of that "effectual fervent prayer" which "availeth much" has induced conditions that, reacting upon certain persons chancing to be in rapport with, and susceptible to, the influence of this particular magnetic field, suffice to produce palpable physical effects in correspondence with the aspirant's desires.

Three visits to S. Winefride's Well are prescribed by the tradition as desirable for seeming a remedy for any ill. Thrice is the prepared pilgrim directed to pass through the healing stream that, thereby, as may be assumed from the symbolism of the act, he may be made whole in his triple parts of body, soul and spirit. And I, a mere casual visitor and spectator there "in this unbelieving generation," reflecting upon my unpremeditated actions during a recent holiday, recall that, moved by what I saw and heard and read of it, upon three successive occasions I was drawn to visit the Well, in the hope of rending the veil of outward appearances and plucking out the heart of its inward mystery. In what is here written to that end I may or may not have succeeded; but if to S. Winefride or her legend I have done any violence, may she, "still miraculous," pardon the offence for its good motive of directing attention to an ancient shrine and endeavoring to determine the value of a charming and an impressive story.

Walter L. Wilmshurst

SPURIOUS ECSTASY AND CEREMONIAL MAGIC

THE strongest evidence of man's dissatisfaction with his present status and surroundings is furnished by his desire to transcend the drab routine of life and to escape from himself. The yearning for *ec-stasis*— the desire to *stand out* beyond his physical limitations—manifests in many ways. Some of these—conventional amusements, aesthetic or religious emotionalism—are innocuous enough, but when they enter the region called occult, many become wholly evil even when initiated with good intentions, whilst one only is otherwise than entirely spurious, transient, and imperilous. Of the evil methods, it may be premised that they are the shadows and perverted forms of the wholesome way; the homage of imitation and imperfection that vice pays to virtue and its attainment. The vulgar drunkard, for instance, enters after his own manner a spurious temple of the Mysteries to seek the joys of the pothouse, and his cup runneth over as surely, if in a grosser fashion, as his who is inebriated by the mystic Grail in the sanctuary of his own soul. The exhilaration of the aviator is a low-grade replica of that of the religious aspirant who, sighing for the wings of a dove, learns to soar—*superasque evadere ad auras* **(to the upper air)**—otherwise than in modern airships. But the mild delights of the bottle and the thrills accruing from venturesome sports pale to nothingness before the gorgeous illuminations of consciousness inducible by certain drugs and anesthetics. Few, however, care to undertake the experiences of the opium and hashish eater in view of the reaction and inexorable penalty exacted by outraged Nature from those who willfully or through moral infirmity explore the caverns and abysses of the subliminal mind. Of recent years experimental psychology has probed this matter, and Professor James has described very graphically the effects upon himself of intoxication by nitrous-oxide gas. There is produced, he says, an intense and rapturous metaphysical illumination in which truth lies open to the view in depth beneath depth of almost blinding evidence; where subject and object, *meum* and *tuum*, the center and periphery of things, become one; and where one becomes consciously blended with the Infinite. Important philosophical deductions result from these experiments and a treatise upon The *Anesthetic Revelation* by an American citizen is, in its way, of undoubted educational value. But what is the effect of these practices upon the personal organism of the experimenter? It will vary in individuals proportionately to their native moral or immoral condition, and it may be assumed that in the morally degenerate, the results would be much more appalling than those attending alcoholic delirium. But even the average clean-minded man, actuated by the good motive of scientific inquiry, testifies in the person of Professor James himself that he is left with "the sense of a dreadful and ineluctable fate; a pessimistic fatalism; depth within depth of impotence and indifference; . . . terminating either in a laugh at the ultimate nothingness, or in a mood of vertiginous amazement at a meaningless infinity." So far, then, so bad; even at the best. The immature Icarus flying to the sun, gets his wings scorched for his pains and falls back into a sea of trouble.

The Sabbatic Goat.

Contraband illuminism is obtainable also by certain oriental *yoga*-practices and by the frenzy of the dance as exemplified by the whirling dervish who performs his gyrations with the object of deadening the senses and awakening higher centers of consciousness than those to which the senses are the portal. The dance has been used in the rites of sanctity, and perhaps even in connection with the Christian Mass; but it has also served in the mysteries of iniquity as a sensuous and illicit attempt to capture elements latent in the depths of human nature to the legitimate possession of which that nature has not yet attained. This latter was the classic sin of Prometheus in stealing the Divine Fire and using it for carnal ends. But it is perhaps little known that the excitation of psychic passion and the promoting a spurious ecstasy by unlocking an imprisoned essence which, by its proper user, may be suffered to act as the purifier and baptizer of the lower nature, is illustrated, beneath a thick veil of dramatic imagery, in the biblical reference to the lascivious dancing-woman whose object was to reduce into possession of what is figuratively described as "the head of John the Baptist in a charger."

The practices of Theurgy and Ceremonial Magic are cognate in character to those already named. At their best (if the epithet be not an abuse) they are attempts, under cover of pseudo-dedications of sanctity, to stimulate and exercise occult faculties by constraining to the ends of selfish gratification sub-human intelligences and forces that mercifully remain unmanifested to our ordinary perceptions; at their worst, and even at a stage far anterior to that, they are unnameable abominations. As one of the great series of studies upon the varied manifestations of the Secret Tradition in Christian times upon which Mr. A. E. Waite has now for long been engaged, we have before us an elaborate volume, The Book of *Ceremonial Magic*, a most comprehensive treatise in that it supplies the texts of all the chief magical rituals extant, describes the methods and operations, and supplies much historical and critical commentary.

But the author's avowed purpose being to show that Magic, Sorcery, Necromancy and their cognates are perverse corruptions and fungoid growths upon a body of doctrine that is high and holy, the book is negative rather than positive in value; its motive is that of the Spartan fathers when they paraded drunken helots in the presence of their sons; namely, to show them something well worth avoiding. That definite results accrue from magical practices is of course indubitable, but if from following them one were to gain the whole world, or even an inconsiderable portion of it, there is probably no surer way by which to disintegrate eventually one's own soul. It is significant that these operations demand from their devotees preparations as arduous as, and certainly far more ingenious and troublesome than, are required from those who aim at that genuine occult wisdom of which art-magic is the complementary foolishness. The doctrine of both prescribes rigorous discipline of body and mind, but whilst in the one case the end proposed is that of assisting the Divine in man to find its rest in the Divine in the Universe, in the other it is to provoke auto-hypnosis and self-hallucination, to indulge in vanity and self-glory, to truckle with obscene powers, to steal nefarious marches upon and influence the freewill of one's neighbor, and to obtain abnormal facilities for practicing lewdness unperceived. *Corruptio optimi pessima* **(The corruption of the best is the worst)**; or as S. Francis of Sales once said in taking the pure and sweet scented lily as the symbol of the perfected soul, 'there is no scent so foully malodorous as that of rotten lilies'. Mr. Waite has performed a considerable service, though doubtless a disagreeable task, in collating the literature of Ceremonial Magic, in indicating its methods and aims, and especially in demonstrating the invalidity of the distinction popularly made between magic that is thought to be White and that which is admittedly Black. It is perhaps too much to hope that efforts towards attaining artificial illuminism or that the prostituted use of occult powers will cease to be made as the result of this volume, but, so far as literature can pronounce it, for all but the ignorant, the imbecile, or the wantonly wicked, this book is as the Last Judgment thereupon.

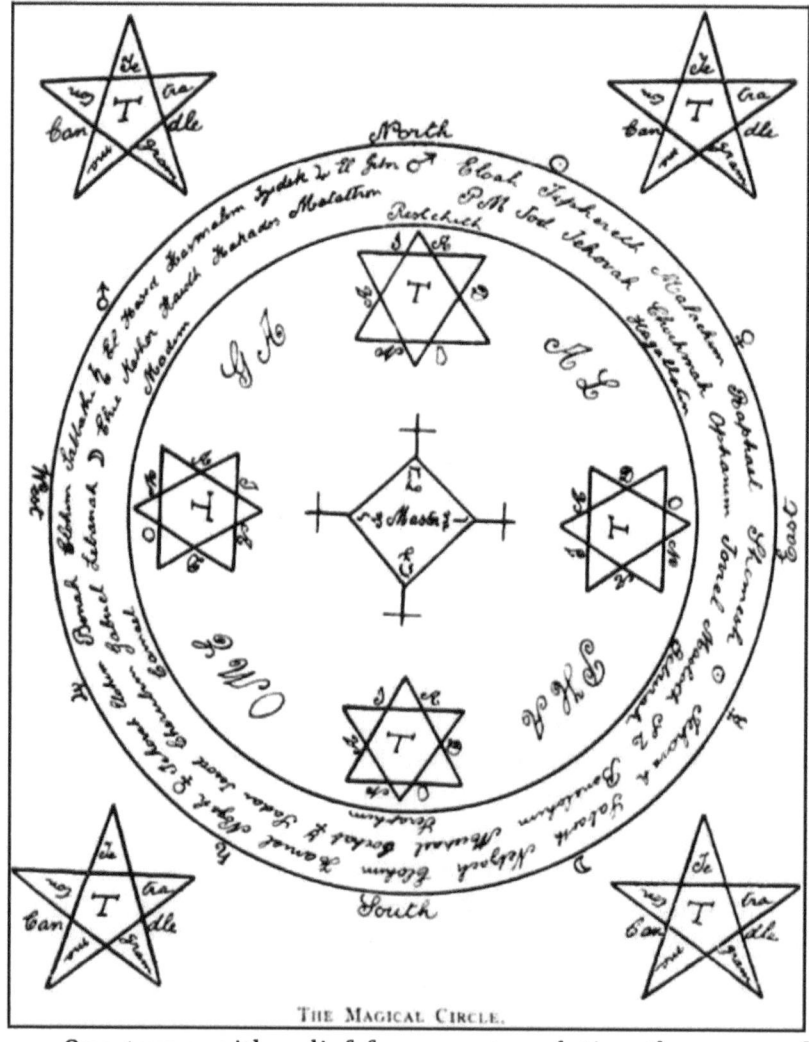

THE MAGICAL CIRCLE.

One turns with relief from contemplating the ways of vanity and evil, to the one remaining path leading to the true ecstasy and veritable Magia; the path which I have said above is alone legitimate and safe as it alone is to be computed genuine occultism and the only one worth any one's while to pursue. Given the fact, which lies at the basis of all occultism, that high and hidden centers of consciousness and power exist sealed up within the human organism, there exist also alternative ways of unlocking them. One is by forced, illicit methods conducing inevitably to mental and moral disintegration; the other is by a "graduated fire" and methods inducing legitimate and normal growth towards, and ultimate absorption in, the focal source and holy center of all consciousness and power, where, voided of all vain desires and in utter immunity from any peril, the soul, *In the ultimate Heart's occult abode May lie as in an oubliette of God.*

GOËTIC CIRCLE OF PACTS.

As regards the former of these methods the best of all authorities stigmatized as thieves and robbers those who sought to "climb up into the sheepfold by some other way" than that of growth in grace and sanctity and through the strait gate and narrow way prescribed by the law and the order; whilst a lesser one who learned the Secret Doctrine independently of the Christian fold has also testified that those few who find the hidden door legitimately are such as have been found specially worthy to be interiorly illumined or have won their title to the heights by an inflaming passion for holiness;

> *Pauci, quos acquus Acqua Jupiter,*
> *aut ardens evexit ad aethcra virtus,*
> *Dis geniti potuere*

(Very few, to whom Acqua Jupiter loved, or whom burning virtue lifted up to the sky just a virtue, the gods were able)

I will add but one word, lest Mr. Waite's new volume should by any be thought negligible because it treats of a subject that is so. In a succinct and powerful introduction, he has himself provided the antidote and counter-thesis to the main subject-matter of his book. No terser summary, yet no more explicit and luminous exposition of the one legitimate occult path, as often defined and often traversed during the age of Christendom, has, to my knowledge, appeared in public literature. And at a time when many minds are seeking for sound counsel and feeling after the true way, and yet when, to meet this demand, glittering temptations exist to divert them towards spurious and dangerous processes, Mr. Waite's introductory pages to the collated records of pseudooccultism come as a warning to inexperienced aspirants and as a trumpet-challenge that says, "Choose ye this day whom you will serve!"

THE SECRET DOCTRINE IN ISRAEL

ALTHOUGH the great public is unconscious of the fact, and professional theologians ignore it, for the minority of those interested in the byways of religious thought and history it remains an unassailable fact that, concurrently with the public doctrine accepted of the masses in any given age, an inner and deeper doctrine has been held and practiced by a few who, intellectually or spiritually, have outgrown the elementary public presentation of religious truth. This more withdrawn teaching, with the practices it has inculcated for advancing personal progress in the spiritual life, has come to be called the Secret Doctrine, or the Secret Tradition. It has undergone many changes of outward expression, but its central tenets have remained the same, for in the nature of things the ultimates of religion must necessarily be immutable (indeed this is affirmed daily in Christian Churches when the words are uttered. "As it was in the beginning, is now, and ever shall be"), and the student of comparative religion has no difficulty in penetrating the varying veils of expression and identifying the underlying principles.

The suggestion that there is, or can be, secrecy in regard to spiritual truth and matters which, if momentous at all, are of common moment to all and ought not to be the privilege of a few, is sometimes resented by the modem mind as both presumptuous and offensive. The objection is unsound, and slight reflection will show that the secrecy in question is inherent in the nature of things and is due to force of circumstance rather than to arrogance or affected superiority on the part of a minority towards a majority. Qualification for the knowledge of something richer and fuller than popular exoteric doctrine provides is, and has always been, a matter of personal fitness for, and ability to appreciate and assimilate, it; and other qualification, there is none. The old maxim applies that when the pupil is ready, the teacher is found waiting for him, and he passes on to the knowledge of things that have previously been concealed from him simply because he lacked both desire and aptitude for them. The Grecian Mysteries were certainly always secret, yet the fact of their existence was a matter of public knowledge and there was no more secrecy about their sanctuaries than there is about a modern cathedral; their presence testified to the public that a deeper than the popular religious doctrine did exist, but the right of admission and initiation into them depended upon the aspirant's wholehearted desire to associate himself with what those Mysteries involved. And the same qualification has obtained elsewhere in regard to subsequent expressions of mystical religion, of whatsoever formal expression, and whether formally organized or not. From time to time in these pages I have drawn attention to the veritable and valuable opus magnum undertaken by Mr. A.E. Waite in summarizing and collating the various forms into which the Secret Doctrine (in regard to cosmogonical truth and the reintegration of human into divine nature) has passed, so far as available records render that task feasible. His Real History of the Rosicrucians, his *Hidden Church of the Holy Grail*, his *Book of Ceremonial Magic, and his Secret Tradition in Masonry*, have been severally chapters in one long story of the forms that Doctrine has assumed under the Christian aegis, and now to the series he has added The Secret Doctrine in Israel as a summary of it under that of Jewry. For, notoriously, Judaism possessed its withdrawn esoteric side and oral tradition (the Kabbala), as well as its exoteric church and public scriptures. What the mystical Taoist was to the Confucianist, what the Sufi was to the average Mahommedan, what the Christian mystic and contemplative has been to the nominal religionist of our dispensation, that the "Sons of the Doctrine" (as the Jewish mystics were called) were to the average exoteric Hebrew. In the nature of things—since no records exist of a purely oral doctrine—we can never know fuller details of the

Secret Doctrine in Israel, as it flourished in its prime in pre-Christian times, than the traditions and hints of it to be gleaned from the post-Christian Kabbalists. But (though the subject cannot be enlarged on here) there is good reason for supposing that it was from the now unknown and saintly mystics of Jewry, who for generations had dedicated themselves and prepared the way for the Messianic manifestation, that eventually and in the fullness of time the desire of nations did forth come in the person of Messias "which is called Christ." With that eventuation the withdrawn school of Jews (using that term in the apostolic sense that "he is not a Jew who is one outwardly, but who is one inwardly" and mystically) seems to have achieved its purpose as an organic instrument for furnishing the "body prepared" through which the Christian evangel was given to the world, and what remained over for after-years was but the afterglow of a great and glorious assembly, the light of which had long existed in concealment whilst its shadow had been the official system of exoteric Judaism.

The pursuit of the Secret Doctrine thereafter continued, and eventually oral Kabbalism, or some portions of it, passed into writing, and from its surviving remnants it is possible both to deduce something of what the Tradition was, and to learn the extremely mystical nature of the exegesis accorded to the Scriptures of the Law. But the period from which any records of it date was one of declension compared with that which had anteceded it. From this latter period date, the treatises and records of Rabbinical conferences that, in their collected, but chaotic, form constitute that storehouse of Kabbalism, the *Sepher-Ha-Zohar*, or *Book of Splendor*. Save for a few fragments unsatisfactorily reproduced from Rosenroth's Latin version, it has never been translated from original Chaldaic into English. A French translation by M. Jean de Pauly in six substantial volumes has been issued in recent years, and it is from this that Mr. Waite has been able to summarize and coordinate the chief features of Rabbinical mystical wisdom so far as written memorials enshrine it. Only by reference to his volume can an idea be formed of the enormous labor and research entailed in its compilation. Only to one endowed with great gifts of scholarship would such a work be possible, and only by one thoroughly and sympathetically familiar with mystical religion generally would such an effort have been thought worthy of execution or could its accomplishment have been made of value to students interested in this region of research.

What is now laid open to the English reader is an epitome of the central principles and ideas of Kabbalism—so far as the Zohar and its connections reflect the doctrines of that school—and it is vouched by innumerable references to the text, and supplemented by connective, illuminating commentary by Mr. Waite himself, whose previous studies in other forms of the Secret Doctrine have enlarged his qualifications for interpreting the expression of it that obtained in Israel. The wide range of Kabbalism, and an idea of Mr. Waite's analysis of it, may be gathered from the titles of some of his twenty-one chapters. These include studies of the Doctrine of the Hidden Church in Israel, the Majesty of God in Kabbalism, the Doctrines of Cosmology, the Fall, the Abrahamic Covenant, the Mosaic Law, Eschatology, the Mystery of Shekinah, and—chief of all—the Mystery of Sex. The book concludes with chapters dealing with the merging of Judaism into Christian doctrine and a general view of Jewish Theosophy. For those who may consider as obsolete or negligible the records of a phase of religious expression which has been superseded by that under which we now live, it may be useful to quote Mr. Waite's deliberate judgment that "perhaps at this day it has a greater message for us than it had ever for our brothers in Jewry." There is a sense in which the theosophy of Jewry is dead, but there is another in which it yet lives and speaks loudly, for the undying spirit of it is that which animates the mystical life in all ages, and from the distance of a time long past now comes the corroboration of—nay more, it throws emphatic and brilliant illumination upon—other expressions of the Secret Doctrine with which followers and students of it today are more familiar. Were it for nothing else—and I regret that space permits not of any adequate reference to this or to other important features of the book—it is worthwhile to inform oneself how dominant a place the question and the sacramentalism of sex relations held in Jewish Mysticism. Within the Mystery of Sex, as Mr. Waite shows, all other mysteries were conceived as enshrined and connected.

It is a mystery the lack of recognition of which is forcing to the front today in not a few ways certain problems as to the relations of the sexes, and though the spiritual aspect of the subject is the more impressive and important for the student of mysticism, there is yet an outward and practical side to it, affecting the common relations between man and woman, which leads Mr. Waite to utter the following confession: "I am the last person in the world to enforce practical conclusions, but if those who are prepared thereto within and without were to enter the nuptial state and fulfil it consistently, as also with high reverence, in the sense of the Zohar, I think that the world might be changed, and that a generation to come, born of such unions, would be children of a risen life." Jewish Mysticism, lofty and highly speculative as it was in one of its aspects, was nothing if not practical in its applicability to the primary human relationships—the marital and filial—for it saw clearly that those relationships are the shadow upon earth of realities beyond. I will add but two observations. The first is one of public acknowledgment to the author and publishers of The Secret Doctrine in Israel, for at last making the contents of the Zohar known to us. The other is that orthodox theologians little know what is sealed from them by their failure to give recognition to the stores of light available in the records of the Secret Tradition, whether of Jewry or of Christendom.

Walter L. Wilmshurst

THE DEVELOPMENT OF THE CONFLICT

KNOWLEDGE of the workings of natural phenomena during the last five centuries is responsible for bringing about the conflict between scientific and religious thought; in other words, the acquisition of the principle of cause and effect which accounts for the natural universe has been accompanied by the coordinate elimination of the "supernatural" from its originally large occupation of men's thoughts. Roughly speaking the conflict commenced with the Renaissance and the Reformation, and at the outset it developed slowly and only became particularly acute in cases where outspoken individuals fell foul of the Church. Whilst the Reformation brought about exceedingly valuable results, too much insistence is sometimes made upon the claim that it effectuated the emancipation of Reason. The most that can be claimed for it is the proposal to change masters; from being the slave of the Papacy, the intellect was to become the serf of the Bible, or, to speak more accurately, of somebody's interpretation of the Bible. It was the iniquities and not the irrationalities of the Papal system that lay at the bottom of the revolt of the laity. The abolition of transubstantiation, image worship, indulgences, and ecclesiastical infallibility, gave place to bibliolatry, and new alternatives of theological doctrine which, despite the Reformation, continued to flourish as the fruit of the original supernaturalistic tree. At length broke out the skeptical insurrection of the eighteenth century and the free-thought that was engendered by the French Revolution.

The ethical and intellectual criticism of theology, which after the consolidation of the Protestant sects, had been re-commenced by Hobbes, Descartes and Spinoza, broke out into a fierce flame. Christianity was attacked on all hands. It was subjected to the attacks of Rousseau, to the venom of Voltaire, and the calculations of the French Encyclopaedists it met with the cold shoulder of Lessing and the German Rationalists, and, here in England, with the undisguised infidelity of Bolingbroke and Tom Paine, the sly sneers of Gibbon, and the deductions of numerous other philosophers who appealed to the free thought of those days by contending that belief in the supernatural, in revelation, and particularly faith in miracles, were unjustifiable on a priori grounds; in other words, that the so-called miracles upon which Christianity is so largely based were impossibilities, and therefore the whole system was to be rejected as unreasonable. On the other hand, orthodoxy received assistance from eminent apologists, in particular from Bishop Butler, whose "Analogy" dealt a mortal wound to the current speculative infidelity, which, though it claimed to be founded in Reason, was in the light of countercriticism demonstrated to be unphilosophical, irrational, and unscientific. And so the controversy became gradually lifted into the plane with which we today are familiar. The *a priori* method of attack upon Christianity gave way to David Hume's more cogent argument, which alleged not that miracles were antecedently impossible, but that the evidence in favor of them was altogether inadequate to support the claims made on their behalf; the progress of the historical and psychological sciences brought to light the important part played by the mythopoeic faculty and the extreme readiness of men to impose upon themselves. Philologers, biblical critics, geologists, biologists, and archaeologists, working in their respective departments, and applying really scientific methods of seeking for truth, all contributed to widen the issue, to separate the natural from the supernatural, to sever ethics from religion, and to reject as false knowledge the cardinal facts of the Christian faith. "The stream of tendency" (claims one who has been in the forefront of the fight) "towards Naturalism has of late years flowed so strongly that even the Churches have begun, I dare not say to drift, but at any rate to swing at their moorings. Within the pale of the Anglican establishment, I venture to doubt whether at this moment there are as many thoroughgoing defenders of 'plenary inspiration' as there were timid questioners half a century ago. Commentaries sanctioned by the highest authority give up the actual historical truth of the cosmogonical and diluvial narratives. University professors of deservedly high repute accept the critical decision that the Hexateuch is a compilation in which the share of Moses, either as author or editor, is not quite so clearly demonstrable as it might be; highly placed Divines tell us that the pre-Abrahamic Scriptures may be ignored; that the Book of Daniel may be regarded as a patriotic romance of the second century B.C.; that the words of the writer of the fourth Gospel are not always to be distinguished from those which he puts into the mouth of Jesus. Conservative but conscientious reviewers decide that whole passages, some of dogmatic and some of ethical importance, are interpolations. An uneasy sense of the weakness of the dogma of Biblical infallibility seems to be at the bottom of a prevailing tendency once more to substitute the authority of the Church for that of the Bible." But in the words of the same perspicacious writer in summing up the position:

"The antagonism of science is not to religion, but to the heathen survivals and the bad philosophy under which religion herself is often well-nigh crushed. And for my part, I trust that this antagonism will never cease; but that, to the end of time, true science will continue to fulfil one of her most beneficent functions, that of relieving men from the burden of false science which is imposed upon them in the name of religion."

Now let us see what, after exercising their destructive criticism, the apostles of natural science propose to put in place of the theological doctrines they have attacked. There have been a good many of them, and they by no means all agree in the same conclusions, but for the present, we will be content to consider the *dicta* of a few of the most conspicuous and representative among them. No sooner had modern science ravaged the territory of the theologians than her leaders began at once to coordinate the knowledge they had won, and to deduce certain conclusions of their own. In other words, they began to adopt the very methods they complained of in the theologians. They became dogmatic. The happy wit of the Bishop of Ripon has illustrated the position by likening Religion and Science to two grave and peaceable old ladies living in different stories of the same house. Religion had a daughter named Dogma, and Science one called Theory, and whilst the parents could easily have managed to live on most friendly and peaceable terms, yet whenever their offspring met upon the staircase wrangling and discord at once began.

Then Dame Science came out of her room and called Miss Dogma hard names, alleging she was no better than she should be; whereupon Mistress Religion emerged from her parlor and retorted upon her neighbor that Miss Theory was, to say the least, no more genteel than Miss Dogma, and that if the latter young lady had been caught tripping now and then, the same objection could be applied to the other. For the theories of Science, like the dogmas of Theology, are mere working hypotheses; conclusions drawn from certain premises, and capable of adjustment to the demands of increased knowledge as knowledge itself increases. Gravitation cannot be proved any more than the Incarnation; evolution is an inference as much as the doctrine of the Trinity; the ether a postulate as necessary a basis for scientific thought as the existence of a Deity is a basis essential to the practice of religious thought. In each case, certain assumptions are necessary, and these assumptions may differ at different times, but in any case, Science is as dogmatic as Theology, and Theology as theoretical as Science; and no finality is practicable for either.

Let us then examine some of the dogmatic conclusions in regard to matters of religion as they have been put forward by modern scientists. The extreme wing is, perhaps, to be found in the school of German Materialism, whose policy is one of war to the death with everything theological. Science, it claims, has advanced along a hundred paths, in astronomy, geology, biology, psychology, ethnography, history, ethics, and comparative religion, and all its lines converge fatally and irresistibly on one conclusion—the utter exclusion of theology from the domain of cosmological theory. "Science has conducted God to its frontiers, thanking Him for His provisional services," is the arrogant claim that has been made. What then are we to substitute for Him? What is there left for us to believe in? Answers are to be found in the works of such representative writers as Professors Ludwig Buchner and Ernst Haeckel, and, summarized, they are as follows: There is nothing in the universe but Matter and Force. All the phenomena of Nature are explicable by deduction from the properties assignable to these two primitive factors, which are the Alpha and Omega of existence. To be quite fair to the exponents of these views, however, they disclaim the title of Materialists. They prefer the title of Monists, and for this reason. All the philosophical tendencies of the past tend to be either dualistic or monistic. Dualism breaks up the universe into two entirely distinct factors: the material world and an immaterial God. Monism, on the contrary, recognizes one sole substance in the universe which is at once God and Nature. Body and spirit, it holds to be inseparable; matter cannot exist without spirit, nor spirit without matter. Life, the Monists say, is not itself matter, but the outcome of a long series of processes which have led to the appearance of matter in its organized condition; a form of activity, like heat or electricity; something that ceases to exist in the individual at the stage of natural progress, which we call death. Consciousness, apart from a material brain, is an impossibility, and to think of a personal Deity "gives us the paradoxical picture of a gaseous vertebrate."

Belief in immortality is the very citadel of superstition; for we are nothing but the perishable children of the earth who for a few years have the good fortune to enjoy the treasures of our planet, to trace out the marvelous play of its forces until their inexorable machinery grinds us once more into unconsciousness and indestructible dust. There are not two different, separate worlds, one physical and material, the other moral and immaterial. The only ethics available for us is to live in complete harmony with the monistic aspect of the universe and obey the Golden Rule, which, apart from any sanction of religion, is dictated by universal human experience as the highest ordinance of human conduct. But whatever we know or ever can know, however deeply we may probe and unfold the secrets of Nature, matter is the terminus to which all knowledge and research must lead; in the light of which everything must be considered.

All thought, all emotion, all imagination, all aspiration, whatsoever things are high or good, or worthy to be believed, all life and the attributes of life are but manifestations of "the simple monistic basis of all things which remains one and the same in itself throughout all the changes and diversity of its phenomena. When this faith shall have conquered there will be an end of the old unscientific depreciation of matter, and the world of the long misunderstood and despised materialist will be grander and nobler than any of the imaginative and artificial structures of the theologian and the philosopher." I wish to be quite fair in stating the views of other people and in making this brief and inadequate exposition of the Materialistic or Monistic system, the brevity and inadequacy may perhaps be forgiven for the reason that the system is not difficult of apprehension. The application of the touchstone of a single principle—the eternity of matter and the perpetual conservation of force—to all subjects of acquired and potential knowledge and the ruthless elimination of all belief in anything wherein the sequence of cause and effect cannot be traced, make the position of its formulators perfectly clear.

The system is based upon the principles of pure reason defined by the critical Kant. It implies—what Kant denied and what has become the very foundation of all critical, as distinct from idealistic, philosophy—that human faculties are capable of apprehending the ultima ratio of the Universe and into its philosophy the three great central dogmas of metaphysics—a personal God, free will, and the immortal soul—which "the dogmatic" Kant was driven to admit into his system of practical reason, have no place whatever. It emphasizes the theory that matter is spirit and spirit matter, but, in making the assertion, the stress is upon the term matter, spirit being apparently an *ex gratia* admission into the formula, for spirit in its judgment is merely a figment, a metaphysical phrase denoting something non-existent, or, at best, conceivable only in terms of matter. The distinction is important, as we shall presently have to consider the question, which must already have suggested itself. What, after all, is Matter? An alternative doctrine of a less presumptuous and uncompromising kind is offered to us by the thought of Herbert Spencer. Instead of laying down hard and fast limits which the human mind can never under any circumstances transcend, instead of defining precisely the ultimate possible bounds of experience and dictating for universal acceptance doctrines of God and Nature which one must never attempt to exceed on pain of making a fool of oneself, Spencer adopts indeed a positive, but a much more humble, attitude. With untiring patience and skill, he coordinates all the facts of experience; he lays down that for the present we must confine ourselves within the established limits of intelligence; he recognizes in common with the Monists that all phenomena, from their great features even to their minutest details, are necessary results of the persistence of force under its forms of matter and motion, that the rhythm of progress and dissolution runs ceaselessly through every department of the Universe and is one of its fundamental properties. But after applying this touchstone to things capable of human experience he, with equal courage and clearness of vision, asserts and justifies his position as a Dualist, and affirms that when all is said that can be said of the objective or "knowable" Universe, there is still a vast immaterial realm to which principles of pure reason are inapplicable. He admits the general probability that widely-spread beliefs are not absolutely baseless; that the existence of religious sentiment, whatever its origin, is a fact of great significance, and that as knowledge cannot monopolize consciousness, it must always continue possible for the mind to dwell upon that which transcends knowledge. Hence, there must always be a place for Religion, which under all its forms is distinguished from everything else in that its subject-matter is something that passes the sphere of ordinary experience. Science, on the other hand, is simply the higher development of common knowledge. But if both Religion and Science have bases in the reality of things, then between them there must be a fundamental harmony. There cannot be two orders of truth in absolute and everlasting opposition.

To understand how Science and Religion express opposite sides of the same fact, the one it's near or visible side, the other its remote or invisible side, is our problem. How to find this harmony, how to reconcile the two, is the question to be answered. We have to seek out that ultimate truth, which both will avow with absolute sincerity. But, he says, if the two are to be reconciled, the basis of reconciliation must be this deepest, widest, and most certain of all facts—that the Power which the Universe manifests to us is utterly inscrutable, a proposition which, though often contravened by the anthropomorphism of unimaginative religious teachers, is none other than the doctrine of the Incomprehensibility of God affirmed by the professions of faith of Christendom. And so, with all humility and reverence our great English thinker, in his desire to summarize experience and elucidate the laws and principles regulating terrestrial life, if haply he might thereby make a little clearer the complexities of our existence and dispel error and reduce suffering by giving us surer knowledge (which is the true end of all philosophy), was driven by the very nature of his argument to point with no uncertain finger the dividing line between the Knowable and Unknowable. His task—and what a task, and how patiently accomplished—lay in mapping out the processes at work in the Knowable. The Unknowable he did not presume to meddle with; indeed, in the nature of things, and in the nature of his own adopted methods, it was beyond the compass of pure reason; but he tells us plainly that his reasoning's afford no support to either Materialist or Spiritualist respecting the ultimate nature of things, and that though the relation of subject and object renders necessary to us the antithetical conceptions of both spirit and matter, the one is no less than the other to be regarded as but a sign of the Unknown Reality which underlies both. How far Spencer was justified in defining the Unknowable depends on the limitations attached to the term knowledge; and how far and in what various ways a human mind may know things coming within Spencer's category of the Unknowable is an interesting question to be referred to a little later on. But his predication of the Unknowable leads us to a third type of thought which, whilst accepting the Spencerian system in the main, has dissociated itself from this particular tenet of Spencer's. It is the type of which no better example can be found than Professor Huxley. And let me premise my reference to and ultimate disagreement with Huxley's attitude by saying in sincerity and without the least desire to speak patronizingly of so great a man, that in this bitter conflict between Science and Religion, Huxley has, in my judgment, done more service and assumed a more reasonable attitude than any of his fellow polemists. He has been in England the gladiator-in-chief on the scientist's side. Endowed with powers of expression of great lucidity and exceeding trenchancy, always absolutely honest to himself and studiously fair to others, he has demolished false scientific reasoning as impartially as he has attacked dubious theology.

Walter L. Wilmshurst

Agree with or dissent from his conclusions as we may, it may be affirmed that he has done more, perhaps, than any man in clearing the ground, and if he never arrived at the ultimate truth he so ardently fought for, he made the way plainer for others to follow; he put his opponents on their mettle, and aroused activities that might have remained dormant but for him; a man like Spencer, distinctly to thank God for. Huxley preferred not to go so far as Spencer; he was content to be even less dogmatic. The hardest of hitters, he always made sure of his ground before he struck. "I do not very much care," he says, "to speak of anything as 'unknowable.' What I am sure about is that there are many topics about which I know nothing and which, so far as I can see, are out of reach of my faculties. But whether these things are knowable by anyone else is exactly one of those matters which is beyond my knowledge, though I have a tolerably strong opinion as to the probabilities of the case." He expressly admits that the scientific Naturalism of modern times does not lead to the denial of the existence of any Super nature, but simply to the denial of the validity of the evidence at present adduced in favor of this or that extant form of Supernaturalism. His claim for Science (and it is much less pretentious than that put forward by the school of Haeckel) is that she is modestly conscious of her ignorance of the high matters propounded by religious teachers. Like Cinderella, "she lights the fire, sweeps the house, and provides the dinner, and is rewarded by being told that she is a base creature devoted to low and material interests. . . . But she sees the order which pervades the seeming disorder of the world; the great drama of evolution, with its full share of pity and terror, but also with abundant goodness and beauty, rolls before her eyes, and she learns, in her heart of hearts, the lesson that the foundation of morality is to have done once and for all with lying, to give up pretending to believe that for which there is no evidence, and repeating unintelligible propositions about things beyond the possibilities of knowledge!"

He expressly dissociates himself from the out-and-out Materialism of the German type. "I understand the main tenet of Materialism to be that there is nothing in the Universe but matter and force, and that all the phenomena of Nature are explicable by deduction from the properties assignable to those two primitive factors... But all this I heartily disbelieve. It seems to me pretty plain that there is a third thing in the Universe, to wit, consciousness, which I cannot see to be matter or force, or any conceivable modification of either, and that our certain knowledge does not extend beyond our states of consciousness. All the materialistic writers I know of who have tried to bite that file have simply broken their teeth!"

Nevertheless, whilst denying Materialism, its antithesis, Spiritualism, lands him in even greater difficulties. "For the assumed substantial entity, spirit, which is supposed to underlie the phenomena of consciousness, as matter underlies those of physical nature, leaves not even a geometrical ghost when these phenomena are abstracted.... Spiritualism is, after all, little better than Materialism turned upside down. And if I try to think of the Spirit which a man, by this hypothesis, carries about under his hat, as something devoid of relation to space, and as something indivisible, I confess I get quite lost." What position, then, ought we to take up? Let us hear his own answer.

"When I reached intellectual maturity and began to ask myself whether I was an atheist, a theist, or a pantheist, a materialist or an idealist, a Christian or a freethinker, I found that the more I learned and reflected, the less ready was the answer, until at last I came to the conclusion that I had neither art nor part with any of these denominations except the last. The one thing in which most of these good people were agreed was the one thing in which I differed from them. They were quite sure they had attained a certain 'gnosis'— had more or less successfully solved the problem of existence, whilst I was quite sure I had not, and had a pretty strong conviction that the problem was insoluble... So I took thought and invented what I conceived to be the appropriate title of 'agnostic.' It came into my head as suggestively antithetic to the 'gnostic' of Church history, who professed to know so much about the things of which I was ignorant."

Agnosticism, he goes on to say, is "not a creed but a method, the essence of which lies in the rigorous application of a certain principle... Positively, the principle may be expressed: In matters of the intellect, follow your reason as far as it will take you without regard to any other consideration. And negatively: In matters of the intellect, do not pretend that conclusions are certain which are not demonstrated or demonstrable. That I take to be the agnostic faith, which if a man keep whole and undefiled, he shall not be ashamed to look the universe in the face, whatever the future may have in store for him." Applying this principle to current religious ideals, the whole fabric of the latter becomes demolished, not on a priori grounds of impossibility or incredibility, but from sheer lack of evidence to support it.

A religious system based upon assumptions such as are contained in the Thirty-nine Articles, supported by the supposed occurrence of miracles and fanned by prayer and pietistic emotion, can have no abiding-place when tried by the touchstone of the agnostic principle.

"I repeat that it is not upon any a priori considerations that objections either to the supposed efficacy of prayer in modifying the course of events, or to the supposed occurrence of miracles, can be scientifically based. The real objection, and, to my mind, the fatal objection, to both these suppositions, is the inadequacy of the evidence to prove any given case of such occurrences which has been adduced.... If a man can find a friend, the hypostasis of all his hopes, the mirror of his ethical ideal, in the Jesus of any or all the Gospels, let him live by faith in that ideal. What shall or can forbid him? But let him not delude himself with the notion that his faith is evidence of the objective reality of that in which he trusts. Such evidence is to be obtained only by the use of the methods of science as applied to history and to literature, and it amounts at present to very little."

And then he goes on to point out that

"It was inevitable that a conflict should arise between Agnosticism and Theology, or rather I ought to say between Science and Ecclesiasticism. For Theology the Science is one thing, and Ecclesiasticism—the championship of a foregone conclusion as to the truth of a particular form of Theology (the Ecclesiasticism which says in Dr. Newman's words, 'Let us maintain before we have proved,'—is another. With scientific Theology Agnosticism has no quarrel. . . . The scientific theologian admits the Agnostic principle, however widely his results may differ from those reached by the majority of Agnostics. . . . But as between Agnosticism and Ecclesiasticism or Clericalism there can be neither peace nor truce. The cleric asserts that it is morally wrong not to believe certain propositions, whatever the results of a strict scientific investigation of the evidence of these propositions. He tells us 'that religious error is, in itself, of an immoral nature.' He declares that he has prejudged certain conclusions, and looks upon those who show cause for an arrest of judgment as emissaries of Satan. It necessarily follows that for him, the attainment of faith, not the ascertainment of truth, is the highest aim of mental life. And on careful analysis of the nature of this faith, it will too often be found to be, not the mystic process of unity with the Divine understood by the religious enthusiast, but that which the candid simplicity of a Sunday scholar once defined it to be: 'Faith is the power of saying you believe things which are incredible.' Now and many other Agnostics believe that faith in this sense is an abomination."

OFFICIAL theology which had withstood so many assaults during the last two centuries would have suffered little from the violent iconoclasm of a few modern experts in natural science who ventured to invade ecclesiastical territory, but for the operation simultaneously of a silent and far more subtle influence. Huxley's trenchant diatribes and lucid application of pure reason to religious ideals might have passed with Hume's negations and Voltaire's mockeries into comparative oblivion but for the disintegrating effect of historical and textual biblical criticism emanating from within the theological camp itself; the retort that the cobbler should stick to his last would promptly have been urged by a public little disposed to have its religious views disturbed to the famous biologist who left his polyps and protoplasm to come down into the arena and do great battle with eminent divines, had it not been that the sacred ark seemed in danger even from its own defenders. But if leading scientific laymen could so lay bare the weaknesses in the armor of professional defenders of the faith, how much stronger became the cause of rationalism when theologians and divines clothed with the holy orders of the Church herself and speaking from their academic chairs were seen to be abandoning wholesale tenets that theretofore had been deemed absolutely essential to salvation. Up to the Reformation theological study devoted itself to dogma, and the spiritual life was supposed to be nourished by Sacraments rather than by Scripture. With the revulsion from Rome, the spread of learning, and the printing and distribution of the Scriptures among the masses, the Bible became the eidolon of the Protestant public. A period followed during which bibliolatry was supreme; when the Bible was regarded, not as a collection of literary jewels, selected and strung together with scrupulous care, but as "one entire and perfect chrysolite," a work whose every word and part bore equal value, and wherein was to be found the record of the universe since time began and a compendium of everything worth calling knowledge.

In startling disregard of the injunctions of primitive Christian teachers like Origen, who insisted that the literal sense of Scripture is often impossible, absurd, or immoral, or

Augustine, who taught that "whatever has no proper bearing on the rule of life or the verity of faith must be regarded as figurative," it was to be read from end to end in supposed chronological sequence and construed as a self-sufficient manifestation of divine wisdom, without reference to the significance of any extra-Christian thought and independently of any critical explanation, historical commentary or psychological sidelight, for of itself it was assumed to be, in the most narrow and rigid sense of the term, the revealed and literal Word of God, written indeed by human automata, but composed, dictated, and, as it were, printed and published by a wisdom and an inspiration altogether praeter-human and unimpeachable. So infatuated a fetishism was bound to lead, as indeed it did, to the grossest superstition and religious narrowness, but with the development of the scientific spirit an inevitable and necessary reaction, involving intense bitterness and controversy, was brought about.

Old Testament criticism, dating from 1680 (when a French priest discovering in the text of Genesis two accounts of the same events inferred therefrom at least a dual human authorship of the book) and restricted for 150 years to the timid, tentative questionings of a few solitary students, became at last a definite organized science in the hands of such experts as Kuenen, Wellhausen, Robertson Smith, Canons Cheyne and Driver, to name no others. The New Testament Scriptures were subjected to similar examination by another body of experts, and the evolution of the critical process as it passed through the hands of Strauss and Baur, Rénan and Ritschl, the Révilles and Sabatiers, Schurer and Weizàcker, Harnack and Loisy, is a long history in itself. Meanwhile, Matthew Arnold had added *"Literature and Dogma,"* the most luminous of the many contributions of freelance critics, to the controversy, and under the solvent effect of research and the application of historical and psychological methods to the Scriptures, dogma and doctrine also began to be transformed. "*Essays and Reviews*" and "*Lux Mundi*" in turn appeared amidst storms of protest that have now rolled away. Parts at least of the three great creeds of Christendom are not at the present day immune from challenge by the broader-thinking clergy, and there is a growing inclination among believers to dissociate the historical human Jesus from the Christ of metaphysics and dogma and to re-state Christian doctrine upon the basis of history. The application of the scientific spirit test to biblical literature and theology was instantaneous in its effect. In less than a generation, how great has been the change of attitude! The present writer remembers hearing one of the most erudite of divines (the late Dean Burgon of Chichester), in stipulating for the literal acceptance of Holy Scripture, deliberately lay down that the account of the Creation in Genesis was to be interpreted exactly as it stood, that the days of Creation were seven actual solar days of twenty-four hours each, and that Eden was "no ordinary garden with a wall round it," in which were suddenly deposited the primal types of all organic life; and as I was then a school-boy learning the rudiments of geology and astronomy, which led me to very different conclusions, I have reason to remember being brought at a tender age into very practical touch with the conflict between scientific and religious thought. But what is freely admitted by equally high-placed dignitaries of the Church today?

To condense a mass of critical conclusions into a few words (and if the statement be brief and blunt, it is made in no captious or irreverent spirit) we are told this: that the Creation story is not literally true, but is a piece of Hebrew fancy; that the earlier narratives before the call of Abraham, including the Flood, are of the nature of myths, in which we can distinguish the historical germ; that the Mosaic Law was not the work of Moses; that the Books of Judges, Samuel, and Kings were not literally inspired; that the Chronicles were not fully historical; that the Prophets had no supernatural power of prophecy; that the Song of Solomon is a drama; that Ecclesiastes was not written by Solomon; that Jonah, and Daniel and Job were dramatic compositions of a patriotic or religious nature, and that the Old Testament is "purified folk lore" and presents a low standard of morality; that the traditional authenticity of the Gospels is disputed, and many famous passages in them are interpolations by sub-Apostolic writers, and that many sayings of the Lord, that have been mainstays of hope and comfort to humanity for centuries, clearly bear the impress of a time which He did not live to see. It is not surprising, then, in a recent work, to find such a statement as the following (it is one I should hesitate to make on my own authority, but I take it from a book, written by a conservative apologist, which bears the imprimatur of Bishop Moule of Durham): "It is a well-known fact that the present dearth of candidates for Holy Orders is due, not to the causes publicly put forward, but to the effects of the Higher Criticism in undermining faith in the Incarnation among those who might be expected to offer themselves for ordination. And it would be a rash statement at this moment to assert that the majority of the clergy believe the Apostles' Creed.

The book 'Contentio Veritatis: by Six Oxford Tutors,' bears startling testimony to the extent of the present apostasy." Such, then, has been the effect of the application of modern science and scientific methods of criticism to religious doctrine that has held good for centuries. And the plain man cries out in despair, "What, then, ought I to believe in? Is Christianity as a system of faith, as distinct from a code of ethical principles, at last extinct, and to be relegated to the domain of myths and ancient Pagan faiths?" He sees the spread of freethought even among the ranks of professional teachers of orthodoxy; he has watched the splitting up of

Churches into school upon school and sect upon sect, each claiming for itself some title to special attention either in regard to what it teaches or what it has ceased from teaching. He sees the decay of interest in public worship; and the almost frantic efforts of ministers of religion to induce an indifferent public to come within their tabernacles. He sees in the newspapers, sandwiched among business advertisements, advices of services comprising special musical features and rhetorical displays upon topical and "catchy" subjects; and, upon the walls of places of worship, placards herald the advent of popular preachers to hear whom the public is invited to flock as to a prima donna or a star-actor. The House of Prayer appears, in many cases, to have become a place of entertainment.

The sanctities of religion are exploited in popular works of fiction. New ethical ideas and religious systems are set before us at every turn in the hope, to apply Kipling's expression (itself significant of the public temper), that;

> *It may be they shall give us greater ease*
> *Than your cold Christ and tangled Trinities.*

Rationalist literature, graduating in tone from sober argument to malignant animosity against Christianity, floods our bookstalls and propagates abuse that less than a century ago would have entailed prosecution for blasphemous libel. The creed that has illumined and cheered mankind near a score of centuries, that shone through his art and breathed in his poetry, that hallowed his architecture and inspired his music—is it all being exploded at the touch of fifty years of modern science? It is a sorry picture. There is, of course, another side to it all. And perhaps it is unfair to attribute the decay of faith entirely to the assaults of science, for the prevalence of disbelief among the masses must be accounted for by numerous causes which are undermining the whole of European society with the raw materials of revolutionary movement, of which I will speak later on.

II - THE DEVELOPMENT OF THE CONFLICT

ON a clear appreciation of the position of the conflict at this stage, there appear, then, to be two cardinal issues at stake. First, is there any justification for religion at all?

Are we justified in assuming the existence of a God and in endeavoring to search after and enter into personal communion with Him; or are we to deny His existence, or, at most, to remain agnostic in regard to it; to shut up the Scriptures as worthless authorities upon the subject, to lay aside all current religious ideals as pernicious, and to confine ourselves strictly to living as best we may according to such light as we may derive from studying the operation of purely natural phenomena? That is the first part of the problem. One of the most marked phenomena of human nature, however, is a tendency towards religion, and scientific thought, on being confronted with it, has then to consider how that proneness should be indulged to the best advantage and with the least violence to Reason. Official Christianity, it has asserted, is unreasonable, and accordingly many have forsworn it altogether; many more are indifferent about it; many, again, have abstracted its ethics and observe them as a rule of conduct while ignoring its supernatural claims. Some, indeed, build altars to an unknown or an unknowable God; some, like Cotter Morrison, urge us to discard all ideas of God and addict ourselves to the Service of Man, bidding us not to lift our thoughts above what we positively know. But while Ethical Societies are formed on every hand, they seem to appeal to but a limited, and that an intellectual, number; they do not touch, and are not likely to touch, the masses; and as regards Positivism and the cult of "Humanity," humanity itself seems to have too small an opinion of its own poor merits to set itself up as an ideal to be worshipped or to seek a solution of its perplexities "through Auguste Comte our Lord."

And so after all these unsatisfactory experimentations and attempts to divert the innate religious propensity of men into new channels, the mind reverts to the consideration of the great religious system that has dominated the western world for nineteen centuries, and to which the majority of people still cling, however feebly, despite the storm and stress to which it is being subjected. That system, as Goethe once said, is by far the greatest achievement of the human race. That faith came into existence as a living force, which grew and took possession of the human race, overthrowing every other force with which it came into collision, and eventually revolutionizing the entire character of human thought and energy. The question now is: Is that force expended? If it is, there is an end to the matter. Christianity will go the way of other mythologies, and mankind must build up another religion for itself. But if, as I confidently believe, it is not, then the question arises:

Can Christianity in the face of recent biblical criticism and modern scientific knowledge justify itself as a reasonable creed and be adapted to modern conditions? And that is the second great issue at stake. It goes without saying, I think, that the historic Christ appeals to the great majority of people; their feelings are predisposed towards Him, but their intellect cannot be induced to accept the official dogmas concerning Him. To use Tertullian's great phrase, *Attima naturaliter Christiana* **('naturally Christian soul')**—the true inner self, despite its own ratiocinative challenging's, has an inherent natural bent towards Christianism. It feels the real claims of Christianity to be moral and spiritual, not material nor even intellectual, although it is by a purely intellectual appeal that one of the chief claims becomes apparent. The moral and spiritual claims are apprehensible only by the moral and spiritual part of a man, the part of him that transcends his intellect, and until established by actual experience they seem unreal and unintelligible. But when, supplementing this personal experience, the intellect can look out upon and grasp the great drama of purpose and providence slowly unfolding itself through the Scriptures as they record the myth and legend, the literature and history of a little tribal race, endowed with an innate genius for religion, working its way slowly and stumblingly from barbaric polytheism to a monotheism at first childishly anthropomorphic, eventually sublimely spiritual and philosophical, and aspiring under the influence of its faith to deal with great cosmic problems; as that myth and legend and history converge upon the great culminating Fact of 1900 years ago, and as the significance of that Fact is seen in turn to absorb Hellenic culture and thought, to humble the pride of Roman civilization, to conquer the barbarism of the North and still to appeal to men today—then the whole spiritual and intellectual man is forced into a state of conviction he can never afterwards repudiate.

That conviction will become further assured if happily he be able to discern that the development of the religious consciousness of Israel and its long preparation for the Messiah's advent is the macrocosm and typifies the expansion of his own microcosmic religious consciousness; for Nature, in her patient maturation of life towards a "far-off divine event," has a cunning way of causing her individual offspring of one age to run swiftly over the physiological and mental ground covered by whole races of men in earlier epochs of human growth. That conviction, also, is not shaken but enormously strengthened by researches that end in showing the Scriptures to be at once more intensely human documents and more convincingly of praeter-human genius or by revelations of natural science that provide an intelligible substructure for moral truth which previously has had but intuition for its support; but the period of transition, during which old metaphysical and mystical doctrines that have served their day have to be abandoned or become adjusted to new scientific truth, is unhappily productive of much distress and rancor, and suspicion, to the eyes of the world, is thrown upon what is true and unassailable. The critical intellect cannot appreciate spiritual methods and scoffs at antique dogmas; the religious mind is wont to ridicule the processes of pure reason and spurn its demonstrations. And so the slow frictional process of adjustment goes painfully on. It has given rise to bitter controversy between sincere religionists and equally sincere rationalists. It is with much grief that both the thoughtful religionist and the reverent sceptic must regard certain episodes in the conflict that have occurred even in our day. The orthodoxy that anathematized Darwin with mediaeval opprobrium humiliated itself by giving him Christian burial in Westminster Abbey, and one might readily refer to recriminations, which it is charitable now not to recall, made by eminent divines in regard to scientific conclusions of the last century now finding universal acceptance with their successors,—utterances painful to read, and which it is painful to think we're ever made by Christian clerics.

It is no part of the purpose of this essay to enter into an exposition of spiritual Christianity or to indicate the various paths by which it may be approached in order rightly to apprehend its truths. My task is to deal with the probable effect of more recent scientific discovery upon the future of religious belief, for we have been told that in the future men must live by science and eschew faith. But, as Mr. John Morley once declared, Science, when she has accomplished all her triumphs in her order, will have to go back, when the time comes, to assist in the building up of a new creed by which men can live, and the present-day watcher of the scientific skies already fancies he sees swimming into his ken signs of new factors that will so affect men's views as to lead them out of the arid wastes of materialism and the dark valleys of agnosticism. Were there no other hope, courage may be taken even from the conclusions of Science herself. *Fas est ab hoste doceri* **(One should learn even from one's enemies)**. Let the very law of Science, the principle of perpetual integration and dissolution—manifesting itself with no less assertiveness in the realm of human ideas than in the world of matter—assure us that, as in the history of the past the believing and the scientific eras have succeeded each other as systole and diastole in the progress of human development, so the free-thought and unbelief of our day will, when the time is ripe, be displaced by a new and settled faith, in constructing which Science herself shall have contributed no unimportant materials.

Theology (the term is used in its widest and an unsectarian sense) is undergoing a process of transformation, and the crisis of transformation, the surging of new life-blood through vein and nerve, causes agony though it augurs health. The blood of many martyrs was needed to be publicly spilt to form the seed of the Christian Church; the secret crushing of innumerable hearts, the estrangement of many from old-time ideals, has been the toll levied by the cosmic process before that Church should attain to larger life and strength. Humanity, by educating itself to think scientifically, is putting away the thoughts of childhood and preparing to march forward, braced by the self-reliance that comes of greater knowledge of its surroundings. It is bidding a definite farewell, not indeed to religion, not to thoughts of God, not to the founder of Christianity, whose name, as Emerson once said, is "not so much written as ploughed into the history of this world," but to the mediaeval theological doctrine that in unscientific days was built up around and now obscures the primitive principles of that faith. In place of that once imposing but insubstantial superstructure, it asks for a substantial scientific foundation.

"Religion must indeed be a thing of the heart, but in order to elevate it from the region of subjective caprice and waywardness and to distinguish between that which is true and false in religion, we must appeal to an objective standard. That which enters the heart must first be discerned by the intelligence to be true. It must be seen as having in its own nature a right to dominate feeling and as constituting the principle by which feeling must be judged. . . . Feeling is necessary to religion, but it is by the content or intelligent basis of a religion and not by feeling that its character and worth are to be determined."

It will be our purpose—and a more pleasant one—to consider now how the modern advance in natural science is contributing to the restoration of religious thought and assisting us to a nobler conception of Christianity. For the crisis is over; it was passed when, on matter being scientifically shown *not* to be the ultimate reality, materialism became an impossible and agnosticism an untenable position. There are difficulties yet to be overcome, but the long conflict is drawing to an end. The hand of the Destroying Angel is being stayed; that of the Angel of Revelation has begun to reconstruct. Perhaps it is the same hand at work in both processes.

> *I looked, and lo! 'mid the decay,*
> *The Waster was the Builder too;*
> *And when the dust-cloud rolled away I saw the new.*

III - NEW FACTORS TENDING TO RECONCILIATION

One of the most distinguished scientific thinkers of the day, Sir Oliver Lodge, recently admitted that he himself had emerged and escaped from the other side of the black pit of agnosticism into which people are toppling.

But far from thinking that the wave of agnosticism had spent itself, he expected to see, indeed he rather welcomed, the coming of a wider, louder, and a more blinding flood of agnosticism.... Agnosticism is the pioneer work of a nobler science and a nobler interpretation of religion. Men must learn to doubt before they learn the desire to know, and it is only the misery of agnosticism, which will drive them into other fields of inquiry, fields which some of us think may lead men from faith to knowledge. People do not fully realize even yet the splendid work of Huxley. The agnostics were not building, they were destroying; they were clearing the ground, are clearing it still, that other hands may build other temples on the places they have laid waste. This shrinking and horror are to be welcomed, not deplored. It is good for a man to discover before he goes Upstairs that he has not learned all there is to know in the Universe. It does not do to go into the next world to cock-a-hoop.

Surely a remarkable change has come about when modern science begins to talk about a future life! For I suppose in the judgment of most people, the solution of the question whether human consciousness persists after death would be a great if not a crucial test of the claims of a spiritual religion. If there be no survival of personality after death, one presumes that the New Testament doctrine, for instance, must of necessity go to the limbo of superstitions; there is no other alternative. If on the other hand, survival be a fact, a strong presumption is established in favor of a doctrine that appeals essentially to man's spirituality. Moreover, on taking thought of the matter, it is difficult to escape the conclusion that if survival be a fact, sooner or later that fact will become demonstrated by purely natural science; in other words, that faith in the life of the world to come will become converted into scientific knowledge of the fact. For it is obvious that if a material body at the period of physical dissolution gives off a conscious incorporeal counterpart or spiritual sublimate of itself, that counterpart or sublimate must evolve upon perfectly natural and traceable lines, and be capable of being located and identified in some secret department of nature hitherto unexplored but not necessarily inexplorable. There is no such thing as "super-nature" or "the super-natural."

The Cosmos is a single fact and Nature the totality of things. Certain phenomena may be abnormal because unusual and unexplained, but once they are tracked out and laid by the heels they take their places in human knowledge, and each one brings with it a message of reproach to man for labelling the natural as the super-natural and the knowable as the unknowable. Now the attitude of modern scientific thought towards immortality has hitherto, of course, been antagonistic; first, because immortality has been held to be an undemonstrated fact; secondly, because it was assumed to be undemonstrable; and thirdly, because no probabilities in its favor had been deduced from physical or biological science. Against these arguments, the aspirations and intuition of humanity have been deemed inadmissible evidence, religious teaching worthless, and Scriptural authority absolutely unreliable testimony. Materialists like Haeckel speak of the idea of life after death as the citadel of superstition an assumption born in barbarous and superstitious times and the result of people concluding from dreams that they had a dual and incorporeal nature which seemed sometimes to separate itself from the body.

They contend that consciousness is the totality of cerebral, and therefore of physical, functions, and that when the physical basis of consciousness, *i.e.* the brain, is demolished at the period of death, consciousness itself must ex necessitate cease to exist. Less positive thinkers relegate the matter to the convenient sphere of the "unknowable." Huxley, with his wonted lucidity, puts it in this way:

"As physical science states this problem, it seems to stand thus: Is there any means of knowing whether the series of states of consciousness, which has been casually associated for threescore years and ten with the arrangements and movements of innumerable millions of successively different material molecules, can be continued, in like association, with some substance which has not the properties of matter and force? As Kant said on a like occasion, if anybody can answer that question, he is just the man I want to see. If he says that consciousness cannot exist, except in relation of cause and effect with certain organic molecules, I must ask how he knows that; and if he says it can, I must put the same question. And I am afraid that, like jesting Pilate, I shall think it not worthwhile to wait for an answer."

And the late Professor W. K. Clifford dismissed the question with a flippant epigram:

"The Universe is made of ether and atoms, and there is no room for ghosts." But the brilliant Clifford died, as F. W. Myers remarked, "before he had time to turn over his atoms thoroughly enough to make sure no ghost was hidden amongst them."

Had he lived until today he would have seen vast changes, brought about by more recent research, in the conceptions of both ether and atoms, and learned what some of his successors now recognize and proclaim—the secret that matter is the form by which is perceptible to our limited senses the spirit which permeates and saturates the entire Universe; that matter is a temporary manifestation of spirit, and therefore, in a sense, an illusion which we look upon as in a glass, darkly. In this sense, then, we can afford to be Monists, declaring matter to be spirit and spirit matter, but differing from the Materialists, we lay the emphasis upon the term spirit; matter being the comparatively unimportant factor in the formula. The new factors, then, in the light of which we must adjust our views of nature and religion today, are derived from advanced knowledge in two fields of research, physics and psychology. Physics has been occupied with the ascertainment of hitherto unknown properties of matter and of the ether. "Twenty years ago, it was thought that the atoms of matter were exempt from liability to change. The form of grouping of the material aggregates changed indeed, but, as Maxwell said, the atoms themselves remained constant; they were the foundation stones of the material universe and were perfect in size and number and weight, unchanged and unchangeable; not capable of wear, but as true today as when they were coined at the mint of the mighty Artificer in some inconceivable dawn of creation. Not so. The process of change has been found to reach to these also. Nothing material is permanent.

Millions and billions, aye, trillions of years it might last, but it was slowly changing; not merely the groupings, but the foundation stones themselves. The atoms were crumbling and decaying; must they not also be forming and coming to the birth?"

Such is the conclusion, deduced from the now known phenomenon of the radio-activity and the electronic constitution of matter. We have been driven to recognize its impermanence and mutability. But what is matter, in its primal condition? It has been traced back to the nebulae in the heavens, out of which the stellar systems are formed, but science has not till now ventured to suggest what produced the nebula. Matter, whether in a gaseous or a solid state, hitherto has been reduced by the physicist to a certain number of elements, a number which, as research proceeds, is gradually shrinking, as some of them are found to be combinations instead of elements. Some that were thought to be elements are now found before our very gaze to be transforming themselves into entirely different elements, until the inference stares us in the face that all matter is ultimately reducible to a single base. And whence, what is that base? The suggestion is being made that the invisible ether, which enfolds and permeates the objective universe, is the mother of matter. The theory is being advanced that the tenuous ether itself is atomic, is possessed of density, and is accountable for the phenomenon of gravitation, and that nebulae are formed out of this electro-magnetic entity that fills the universe; and as the nebula resolves itself into sun and planet, and gives birth to organic life, it follows that in the ether is to be found the basis of all the elements known to chemistry, and of all the complex constituents of life. Now if this ether—an entity invisible, intangible, and of such extreme tenuti that our blunt senses cannot manipulate it, but are bound to regard it as a mathematical figment rather than as a substance, and to assume its existence in order to explain the simplest phenomena of light and heat—be the source of the world of matter, who shall say what possibilities lie hidden in that invisible domain from which matter comes and to which it is returning? Creation, then, is always in process. We are vibrating to the waves that beat upon us from the unseen. Phenomena such as electricity and magnetism we know and acknowledge are its manifestations, but may not consciousness and thought, love and hope, and hate and fear, and every quality of the human heart also be its attributes and emanate from it? And behind and within it all is the Power that moves the mechanism of the Universe. We cannot see this, Power; we cannot find it. It is the Inscrutable, the Incomprehensible; but we know that it is there, just as we know that in these forms of ours, these perfect mechanisms called our bodies, there exists a living, conscious, self-acting and controlling power, a spirit which is not the mechanism itself, and which by experience and observation we know to be distinct from the organism. We are not able to penetrate beyond the instrument to its mysterious User, but we know He must be there, and that He is inseparably connected with each and all of us. So after all, perhaps, there is as much truth as fancy in the thought that poets have often employed, that rhythmic vibrations in the invisible can result in the creation of material objects.

The city, in Tennyson's idyll, which became materialized out of musical vibrations, "built to music, therefore never built at all, and therefore built forever," is a true parable of the birth and flux of matter as the result of the pulsations of the Supreme Mind behind it. And when Browning's *Abt Vogler* mused, as he rolled out his organ chords,

> *But here is the finger of God, a flash of the will that can,*
> *Existent behind all laws, that made them, and lo they are!*
> *And I know not if, save in this, such gift be allowed to man,*
> *That out of three sounds he frame, not a fourth sound, but a star;*

IV - NEW FACTORS TENDING TO RECONCILIATION

PSYCHOLOGY with us Western races is the latest born of the Sciences, and so little advanced in its conclusions that it has been said to be only in the same position today that astronomy and chemistry were 400 years ago. Its function is to investigate and coordinate the phenomena of consciousness; a manifestly difficult task inasmuch as it entails the examination of something by the very thing that is examined, namely, the mind itself. A living mind cannot be dissected by the same methods as a material brain; its operations can only be investigated by studying and comparing its phenomena, and by subjecting consciousness to empirical tests. Still, the student in the psychological laboratory meets with as great orderliness and sequence among the facts of emotion, or memory or reasoning, as the physicist in his laboratory, and he finds it to be beyond doubt that there is no event in consciousness, that is, in the spiritual life of man, which does not occur in accordance with immutable laws. Basing his efforts on physiology and the knowledge of the physical mechanism through which human consciousness works, he collects innumerable specimens of human experiences with a view to deducing the common factors. For individual human experiences are partial revelations of the infinite life, and as it is only by the study of many outcrops of rock that the geologist is able to picture the strata beneath the surface, so from the study of many mental phenomena can be predicted something of the universal Mind of which every individual is a participator. And on investigating the phenomena of consciousness with a view, not to resolve the mystery of religion, but to bring so many of them into orderliness that the facts may appeal to our understanding, and in order to ascertain the rationale of religious aspiration, the psychologist finds certain defined lines of growth in religion; that is, towards a religious ideal. He finds them developing at childhood; that they are traceable by very marked characteristics as they pass through the concomitant periods of physiological growth to youth and adolescence, and that they culminate sooner or later as the physical area of brain-centers of consciousness enlarge into the birth of a larger self, of a new and spiritual consciousness of its relation to the universal Mind. An infant knows nothing of mind; its self consists largely in physiological mechanism, and in experiencing physiological sensations it has to traverse in a few years the path which has been passed over by the race in as many million years, and there is something of a miracle in producing in this short time an essentially spiritual life as much above the life of childhood as the complex physiological functioning of a mammal is above that of a protozoon. A measure of spiritual growth is observable in the majority of people.

But some persons seems to have no, or but an uneventful, development; they perhaps never wake up to an immediate realization of religion. But where the development occurs to a marked extent, the individual comes to recognize the circulation of the Infinite Mind through corporate humanity as practically as he believes in the circulation of the blood through the corporeal man; he sees that we are "mortal atoms of an immortal consciousness." Let us take a few concrete instances. The first shall be that of an undeveloped or atrophied consciousness; a type of hard-headed, practical intelligence, capable indeed of steering its way through the lower and everyday channels of worldly life, but as little conscious of spirituality as a brute. I cull it from that epoch-marking work, Professor William James's "Varieties of Religious Experience." The following somewhat inhuman document was written in answer to a series of questions on religious experience submitted for bond fide scientific purposes. The man under investigation replies as follows:

"Religion to me means nothing, and it seems, so far as I can observe, useless to others. I am sixty-seven years of age, and have resided in fifty years, and have been in business forty-five; consequently, I have some little experience of life and men, and some women too; and I find that the most religious and pious people are, as a rule most lacking in uprightness and morality. The men who do not go to church or have any religious convictions are the best. Praying, singing of hymns, and sermonizing are pernicious. They teach us to rely on some supernatural power when we ought to rely on ourselves. I totally disbelieve in a God. The God-idea was begotten in ignorance, fear, and a general lack of any knowledge of Nature; If I were to die now, being in a healthy condition for my age, I would just as life, yes, rather die with a hearty enjoyment of music, sport, or any other rational pastime. As a timepiece stops, we die; there being no Immortality in either case. God, heaven, angels, etc., convey to me no ideas whatever. I am a man without a religion. These words mean so much mythic bosh. There Is no agency of the superintending kind. A little judicious observation as well as knowledge of scientific law will convince any one of this fact ... Mankind is a progressive animal. I am satisfied he will have made a great advance over his present status 1000 years hence. Sin is a condition, a disease incidental to man's development, not being yet advanced enough. Morbidness over it increases the disease. My temperament is nervous, active, wide awake mentally and physically. Sorry that Nature compels us to sleep at all."

As the professor drily remarks,

"If we are in search of a broken and a contrite heart, clearly we need not look to this brother. His contentment with the finite incases him like a lobster-shell and shields him from all morbid repining at his distance from the Infinite."

Now let us imagine a mind undeveloped in religious experience, be it that of a youth or of an adult whose mental growth for some reason has remained atrophied as in the case just quoted, to be brought into contact with some forcible experience or other of sufficient impressiveness and the like of which it has never previously felt. The experience may be one of a hundred different kinds.

It may be one that would affect different natures differently, according to temperament, heredity, or other predisposition, and the resultant change may be gradual or instantaneous. It may be brought about by the influence of art working upon one's aesthetic perceptivities; or by the influence of scenery or the impressiveness of natural phenomena; it may arise through the solution of intellectual difficulties or religious doubt, by bereavement or by shock, or even by enlarged knowledge of human nature and the ways of the world. Most of us sooner or later become broken on the wheel of life by suffering, either in mind, body, or estate. But whatever may be the causal influence, the individual, when he has successfully survived the experience, emerges from it a new man, with higher ideals, a broader charity, and a clearer outlook upon life; he develops reverence, or rather, Goethe's three reverences—reverence for that above him, that within him, that beneath him. Like the Psalmist, he says,

"It is good for me that I have been in trouble, that I may know Thy statutes."

The psychologist recognizes this phenomenon of mental change, and, seeking for a physiological cause for it, finds it in a corresponding development of activity of previously dormant nerve-cells and an increase in the area of the centers of consciousness in the brain. Thus psychological science finds that she has hit upon the phenomenon which the religionist implies when he speaks of a man undergoing "a new birth," of his being "born again of the Spirit." This process is popularly known as "conversion," but it is not limited to changes wrought in the conscience by the appeals of religion in the narrower sense of the term. Any awakening of the soul "from its dead self to higher things," every fresh perception of and aspiration towards what is nobler than oneself marks a stage of growth towards the Ineffable and Supreme. It has no better illustration than the thoughts Kipling has imagined as harbored by a soldier who has gone through and is returning from the South African War. The superb poem, "The Return," should be read in its entirety and studied for the sake of its deep psychological truth.

"Peace is declared, an 'I return To' Ackneystadt, but not the same: Things have transpired, which made me learn The size and meanin' of the game. I did no more than others did, I don't know where the change began; I started as an average kid, I finished as a thinking man."

This, perhaps slum-bred, warrior, transported to the illimitable veldt, goes on to relate the effect wrought on his mind by a larger vision of Nature; the utter silence of the wilderness, the solemnity of the star-splashed nights—"These may have taught me more or less"; the daily scorch of the African sun, the continual contending with huge distances, the face-to-face meeting with men of his race and blood from colonial regions which to him had been but a name, the bustle of the fight, "the pore dead that look so old an' was so young an hour ago"—these and many other new experiences "are the things which make you know," and open the consciousness to the presence of some indefinable spiritual force which is

"So much more near than I 'ad known, So much more great than I 'ad guessed; An' me, like all the rest, alone—But reachin' out to all the rest"

until at last he emerges, inarticulately eloquent, wiser and humbler, purified and exalted, having caught the first glimpses of a Reality higher than he, yet to which by some mysterious tie he is indissolubly connected.

"So 'ath it come to me—not pride, Nor yet conceit, but on the 'ole (If such a term may be applied), The matin's of a bloomin' soul. But now, discharged, I fall away To do with little things again. Gawd, 'oo knows all I cannot say, Look after me in Thames fontein!"

We recognize here—unconcealed, indeed rather embellished, by the slang—evidence of profound truth to nature. This man could never be again quite what he was before his experiences. His brain is bigger, not only metaphorically but literally; for certain dormant cells in it have been stimulated into activity, thereby enlarging his range of consciousness. He has been "born again," through finding his own spirit responsive to a greater spirit which, without his being aware of it, has wrapped him round.

In the case quoted that greater spirit was but the sentiment that binds together the citizens of a terrestrial empire; but, mutatis mutandis, when the individual human mind comes through moral affinity to respond to the vibration of the Infinite Mind, then the owner of it begins to recognize his relationship to God. Science, observing the phenomenon, asserts that the man has achieved an enlargement of consciousness, has given birth to a consciousness of something transcending knowledge; Religion describes it by saying he is "not far from the Kingdom of Heaven." It would seem that the too exclusive and habitual exercise, within narrow limits, of purely intellectual methods is largely accountable for the non-recognition by scientific minds of the reality of religious experience in others. The late Professor Geo. Romanes, in his "Thoughts on Religion," a most significant confession of his own religious growth, writes:

"Never was any one more arrogant in his claims for pure reason than I was, this being due to contact with science, without ever considering how opposed to reason itself is the assumption of my earlier argument as to God Himself; as if His existence were a mere physical problem to be solved by man's reason alone, without recourse to his other and higher faculties. . . . Not so much by any above-board play of syllogism, as by some underhand cheating of consciousness, do the accumulating experiences of life and thought slowly enrich the judgment. But there is an even higher type of developed consciousness, a type as much loftier than the last as the first quoted was below that. It is a condition attained, perhaps attainable, only by a few; a state in which the human consciousness can virtually dissociate itself from the "muddy vesture of decay" which "doth grossly close it in," and dwell for a brief period in the empyrean of the Eternal Mind and commune with it.

Such communion is now explicable on perfectly rational and psychological grounds, though we have been wont to describe it as emotional, transcendental, mystical; to think of it as the product of superheated imagination rather than to regard it as a normal, if unusual phenomenon. Well-known instances of it occur in the cases of St. Paul, Swedenborg, Boehme, and Wesley. Tennyson, in "The Ancient Sage," and some of the Neo-Platonist writers, Plotinus and Porphyry to wit, speak of the occasional withdrawing, as it were, from their bodies of their whole consciousness, of its temporary absorption into the sphere of the spirit that animates the world as our spirits animate our bodies, and of its inability sometimes, upon returning to its ordinary abode, wholly to remember and recount its experiences during its abstraction. Much in the same way, anesthetics are known to detach a man's consciousness from his physical body and place him in surroundings he cannot recall upon resuming normality. Apart from the comparative study of religious experience, psychological science has a great deal to show us in other departments.

Indeed, the more it unfolds its results, the more apparent is our absolute ignorance of the potentialities of mind and of the abysmal deeps of human personality. It is well, and doubtless providentially purposed, that knowledge of the material universe should have preceded investigation of the invisible world, and for this reason the tidal wave of agnosticism is not such a misfortune as one might imagine. We have been walking hitherto in darkness, but now when the darkness is at its blackest, we are beginning to see a great light. A century ago, no one would have believed in the possibility of obtaining such results as we now produce by telegraphy or telephony. Ten years ago, one would have doubted the possibility of communication over thousands of miles without the help of a cable to conduct the electric current. Today, it is a demonstrated possibility that the result can be obtained between brain and brain by the power of telepathy, the process of thought-transference. Just as in the great ocean of ether above us

"Star to star vibrates light; so soul to soul Strikes through a finer element of her own."

Here, as Sir Oliver Lodge says, is the beginning of a wider conception of Science.

"The distance between England and India is no barrier to the sympathetic communication of intelligence in some way of which we are at present ignorant; just as a signaling key in

Walter L. Wilmshurst

London causes a telegraphic instrument to respond instantaneously in Teheran, which is an every-day occurrence, so the danger or death of a distant child, a brother, or husband may be signaled, without wire or telegraph clerk, to the heart of a human being fitted to receive the message."

This borderland between physics and psychology is a theme of stupendous interest and wonder, involving absolutely new conceptions of the structure and capacity of the human mind. To use a rough and ready illustration, the mind may be compared to a gloved hand. Coming into contact with a certain object, one experiences the sense of touch. Strip off the glove and grasp the object, the touch is all the more sensitive; peel the skin from the fingers and expose the nerve-termini, previously covered by the glove and skin respectively, and the sensation will be so acute as to be painful. The ultimate Ego appears to be involved in a similar series of integuments, and as vibrations beat upon it from without, they are carried forward by the vibratory action of the thought-coatings and result in sensation. Ordinarily the various thought-sheaths are tuned unconsciously by habit to a certain pitch, and as they respond to external impressions, we experience only our normal everyday sensations. But when by some such process as suggestion, anesthesia, or self-induced passivity, the vibratory action of one or more sheaths can be suspended, and the others kept active, then impressions foreign to normal sensation can be experienced through the receptivity of the active sheaths, just as one string of a violin touched at one end of a room will awaken the same musical note on the corresponding string of another violin placed at the other end of the room, the remaining strings of both instruments continuing soundless. To put it in another way, just as a beam of white solar light can be split up into a gamut of rays, so the mind can be split up into a gamut of states of consciousness; and just as we know that both above and below each extremity of the gamut of rays constituting the sunbeam there are other rays imperceptible until established by finer means than ordinary perceptivity recognizes, and of infinitely greater potentiality than those with which we are ordinarily acquainted, so there are subliminal and supraliminal departments of the mind capable of registering perceptions and fulfilling functions outside normal experience.

With the knowledge of the powers of these undeveloped faculties, much that is supposed to be mysterious, miraculous and supernatural, becomes perfectly intelligible; with it, one approaches the Scriptural records almost as if they were new truths, and objections to many of the miracles on the ground of impossibility entirely vanish. We recognize how, through our Western methods of life, our practicality and habits of business, and the part we have played in developing the terrestrial world and performing the elementary functions of the race, we have lost sight of and allowed to become atrophied mental faculties known to and utilized in civilizations of antiquity and still known and utilized by many Orientals of today. Huxley might be said to be the scientific Moses of our time. He led skepticism to the confines of a new world of reconstituted religious thought without being permitted to enter it himself. His clear-sighted and insistent recognition of the fact that over and above Kraft und Stoff, the ultimate elements of Force and Matter of Materialistic philosophers, there was a *tertium quid*, to wit, Consciousness, which they ever left out of reckoning and which he himself could not explain, is of the utmost importance. It indicated that he recognized the existence of the unoccupied territory upon which are being erected the abiding-places of more recent explorers. In a remarkable passage, he imagined the possibility of beings rising higher and higher in intelligence, the consciousness ever expanding, and the reaching of a stage as much above the human as the human is above that of the black beetle.

This is not a flight of scientific imagination; it is a description of fact, as is becoming more and more plain in the light of recent research. So also Herbert Spencer, who on being asked how his great synthesis of the workings of the material world would stand if survival after death were to become scientifically established, replied: "Precisely where it does"; implying that evolution in so much of the universe, as he termed "knowable" is so marked a feature as not to discount the probability of its continuance in what he had marked off as at present "unknowable." The question of the persistence of post-mortem consciousness is a deep and difficult one. I cannot dwell upon it here, beyond calling attention to the published researches on the subject by Sir William Crookes, Sir Oliver Lodge and Dr. Alfred Russel Wallace; the Proceedings of the Society for Psychical Research and especially to the luminous and colossal work of F.W.H. Myers on "Human Personality and its Survival of Bodily Death." Of the moral and religious aspect of the subject, I will not speak at all, but the purely scientific consideration of it points unhesitatingly to the fact that in accordance with perfectly natural law, human individuality continues its unintermitted progression after the incident of death. Just as in the realm of pure physics we can watch the decomposition of one form of matter and trace its transformation by some as yet unimaginable chemistry into some other form (for the self-conversion of radium into helium is but an instance of what is presumed to be the property of other kinds of matter), so in the realm of organic life the evidence points to the fact that out of the corruptible body evolves an incorruptible; that the mortal puts on immortality. In some secret plane in the unknown, every experience of the human brain seems to become registered in perpetuity by the delicate mechanism which enshrines the conscious part of man, his persistent, indestructible Ego. Every thought, word and deed proceeding from him throws out, as from a substance electrically energized, its vibrations into the universe around him, and at the period of bodily dissolution, that inmost Ego or soul of man passes by a natural transition out of the tenement that hitherto has held it and stands clothed with the met-ethereal aura that for good or ill it has built up for itself during its span of earthly existence.

"To die is as easy as to be born, and to a little child, the one is as painful as the other," said Bacon; and there should be little intellectual difficulty in assuming that by the very law of evolution, that unerring process which we have learned to recognize and to follow in every other department of thought, human personality is continued into a realm that has hitherto seemed inexploitable but which in the light of research is very real and very near to every one of us.

If modern doubt and skepticism have done nothing more, they have at least resulted in forcing investigation into the sphere of the unknown and demonstrating the fact for which humanity has had no other authority than its own dim intuition and the half-doubted Scriptural assurance that "there is a natural body, and there is a pneumatical (or spiritual) body"; that the first man is of the earth, earthy; that he develops a second man possessing all the attributes of individuality in the world invisible. Doubtless in time, we shall become habituated to this new outlook upon human destiny. We shall modify, if we have not already done so, the obsolete conception of an infinity of bliss or misery, and learn to contemplate the wise and rational order of things in which our personalities are enabled to pass by easy and natural transition into a state where, engaging

> *"In those great offices that suit*
> *The full-grown energies of heaven,"*

they may work out to completeness the law of their being; where imperfections of character may be rectified, and the aspirations of humanity fulfilled; the inequalities of mundane life adjusted; the crooked made straight and the rough places plain. Let me touch for a moment on another subject to which the scientific spirit has been exceedingly antagonistic—

prayer, which Science has derided, failing to see any chain of cause and effect between the uttering of a petition and the happening of an event. There are few people, I suppose, who imagine that underlying so solemn and private a matter as prayer there is a basis of natural law. Investigation is now revealing that it is reasonable to believe in the physical efficacy of prayer and that the antagonism of science has been unjustified.

Eminent scientists boldly express their faith in the power of prayer and say we have not yet even begun to find out what is possible through its medium. Only it must be prayer with the whole soul behind it, convinced of its own strength and perfect as knowledge. There exists around us a spiritual universe, and that universe is in actual relation with the material. From it comes the energy which maintains the material, the energy which supports the life of each individual spirit. Prayer, says Professor James, or the inner communion with the spirit of the higher, be that spirit God or Law or Nature, is a process wherein work can be done and is done and from which spiritual energy flows in and produces effects, psychological or material, within the phenomenal world. Prayer, whether consciously exercised desire or meditative aspiration, so it be of sincerity and absolute freedom from all doubt, which is fatal to it, sends forth vibrations into the great reservoir of intelligence that interpenetrates the visible world and finds there a sympathetic liberation of energy, a responsive vibration synchronous with itself. Here again, then, a perfectly natural and intelligible rule of law obtains, a law absolutely consistent with our knowledge of physics and psychology.

"That the person who prays does not understand the machinery he sets going in no wise affects the result; he may be even an immoral or irreligious person. A child who stretches out his hand and grasps an object by the mere effort of his puny will does not understand the working of his own muscles, nor of the electrical and chemical changes set up by the movement

in muscles and nerves, nor need he elaborately calculate the distance of the object by measuring the angle made by the optic axes. He merely wills to take hold of the thing he wants and the apparatus of his body obeys his will, though he does not even know of its existence. In like manner, the desires of the human mind, so they be morally in harmony with the Intelligence around it and be projected in unwavering assurance of their capability of fulfilment, can be accomplished with the same positive certainty as attends the transmission and receipt of a message by our commonplace methods of electrical communication."

Thus, we have scientific confirmation of the scriptural admonition: "Ask and ye shall have; knock, and it shall be opened unto you." To quote Huxley once more, man plays the game of life with an invisible power. "The player on the other side is hidden from us. We know that his play is always fair, just, and patient. But we also know to our cost that he never overlooks a mistake or makes the smallest allowance for ignorance. To the man who plays well, the highest stakes are paid with that sort of overflowing generosity with which the strong shows delight in strength. And who plays ill is checkmated, without haste, but without remorse. Nature's discipline is not even a word and blow, and the blow first; but the blow without the word. It is left to you to find out why your ears are boxed." The problem for each of us, then, is to find out the rules of the game. If ever a man yearned to discover them, it was the Hebrew Psalmist, with his repeated cry, "O teach me Thy statutes"; and if any one wished to write a succinct epitome of, say, the 73rd or 119th Psalm in modern colloquial language, he could hardly improve upon Huxley's unconscious paraphrase of it just quoted.

Walter L. Wilmshurst

V - THE PRESENT AND THE FUTURE

TO the sensitive religious mind, there may seem a touch of profanity in the manner in which the cold hand and searching eyes of modern scientific thought are analyzing, on the lines I have indicated, matters connected with our deepest and most sacred associations. Yet, Reason being as beneficent and divine a gift to man as Faith, we need not, I think, be ashamed to approach matters that hitherto have been apprehended only by the eye of Faith, with the other great faculty imparted to us. It seems providential or, if you please to use more scientific phraseology, it seems to be in accord with the law of cosmic development, that when one means of apprehending divine truth becomes wholly or in part weakened, another should be forthcoming to assist the failing faculty. But if any apology be needed for the action of modern science towards the deepest sanctities of religion, let it be made in the beautiful words of one of the most reverent of sceptics:

What a fearful time is this into which we poor, sensitive and timid creatures are born! I suppose the life of every century has more or less special resemblance to that of some particular Apostle. I cannot help thinking this century has Thomas for its model How do you suppose the other Apostles felt when that experimental philosopher explored the wounds of the Being who to them was divine with that inquisitive forefinger? In our time that finger has multiplied itself into ten thousand thousand implements of research, challenging all mysteries, weighing the world as in a balance, and sifting through its prisms and spectroscopes the light that comes from the throne of the Eternal Pity us, dear Lord, pity us! The peace in believing which belonged to other ages is not for us. Again thy wounds are opened that we may know whether it is the blood of one like ourselves which flows from them or whether it is a Divinity that is bleeding for his creatures. Wilt Thou not take the doubt of thy children whom the time commands to try all things, in place of the unquestioning faith of earlier and simpler-hearted generations? We too have need of Thee. The martyrs in other ages were cast into the flames, but no fire could touch their immortal and indestructible faith. We wait in safety and in peace so far as these poor bodies are concerned, but our cherished beliefs, the hopes, the trust that stayed the hearts of those we loved who have gone before us, are cast into the fiery furnace of an age which is fast turning to dross the certainties and the sanctities once prized as our most precious inheritance.

But the century of the Apostle of doubt in which these words were penned has given way already to a century which the signs of the times seem to indicate may, before it closes, bear a resemblance rather to the Apostle to whom, rightly or wrongly, is traditionally attributed the authorship of the fourth Gospel, who more than any of his fellows proclaimed the underlying and essential spirituality of God and humanity. For, despite the tenacity to their cause of a few belated Materialists and the halfway-house position of a large number of Agnostics, the undoubted present trend of thought consequent upon recent discoveries of science and criticism is towards an intellectual conception of a spiritual Universe; a Universe of which the visible objective world is but a relatively unimportant part, its material side being but a temporary manifestation to our limited sense-faculties of the Spirit which underlies and informs it; a Universe which is permeated and saturated through and through by an intelligent, beneficent Power which we call God, who rules His creation by Law and nurtures it with Love. What Science has done for Religion, then, is to have presented her with an intelligible sketch of the system and method by and through which the God of Religion works. As F.W.H. Myers well put it,

"the intellectual virtues, curiosity, candor, care, have now become necessary to salvation. These virtues have grown up outside the ecclesiastical pale; Science, not Religion, has

fostered them; nay, Religion has held them scarcely consistent with that pious spirit which hopes to learn by humility and obedience the secrets of an unknown world."

In the rationalistic times through which at present we are passing, it is the custom of orthodoxy to disparage rationalism unduly. The religionist, secure in the folds of his own faith, generally fails to see the advantage that must ultimately accrue from submitting that faith to the most rigorous tests of reason. The rationalist in his eager quest of truth may come to wrong conclusions; he may have accumulated (and I think this is where most rationalists are at fault) insufficient premises of knowledge and experience to enable him to speak with authority upon matters of which religionists are assured; in his shortsightedness, he may deduce erroneous results, but the very fact that he is searching for truth precludes him from indulging in conscious and willful falsehood. If a man have sufficient sincerity of purpose his very skepticism may ultimately lead him to faith. In the earliest infancy of the Christian faith, its exponents in trying, in the teeth of immense obstacles, to nurse their charge into vigor begged that its critics would apply to it the very tests of reason which too often nowadays its professors regard with reprobation. When we consider modern attainments of natural science and compare them with the rudimentary and childish acquaintance with it possessed in the second century, surely one feels a world of pathos on coming across the words of Clement of Alexandria, pleading for the examination of Christianity in the light of reason and science:

"Some who think themselves naturally gifted (i.e., by the possession of faith) do not wish to touch either philosophy or logic: nay more, they do not wish to learn natural science. They demand bare faith alone.... I call him truly learned who brings everything to bear on the truth, so that from geometry, and music, and grammar and philosophy itself, culling what is useful he guards the faith against assault. How necessary is it

for him who desires to be partaker of the Power of God, to treat of intellectual subjects by philosophizing."

And how the pathos is increased a hundredfold, how much more impressive those simple and ingenuous words appear when eighteen centuries later and after an advance in natural science that has brought into use methods of critical thought which have bidden fair to strangle the life out of Christianity, we find one of our leading scientific thinkers declaring today: "Science is accused of stealing the Christ from religion; but science may yet give back to the Churches a greater and a more wonderful Christ than they have yet apprehended."

It seems then, despite the welter of agnosticism and the flood of rationalist literature that encompasses us, that there is setting in from scientific circles a strong current of thought in a direction that will lead to the surer recognition not only of the Deity, but to the reestablishment of belief, deeper perhaps than ever before, in the truth revealed by Christianity. Where the leaders of scientific thought were five and twenty years ago, a great mass of the public are today; where the bellwethers are now pointing the flock will shortly follow. I have referred to the deeply interesting confession of emergence from agnosticism by Sir Oliver Lodge. Equally significant are the conclusions of the late Professor George Romanes, who worked his way out of the depths of atheism into the full daylight of belief, and expanding Bacon's well-known aphorism declared that,

"if a little knowledge of physiology and a little knowledge of psychology dispose men to atheism, a deeper knowledge of both, and, still more, a deeper thought upon their relations to one another, will lead men back to some form of religion, which if it be more vague, may also be more worthy than that of earlier days." And further: *"It is generally assumed that when a man has clearly perceived agnosticism to be the only legitimate attribute of reason to rest in with regard to religion,*

he has thereby finished with the matter; he can go no further. Such is by no means the case. He has then only begun his inquiry into the grounds and justification of religious belief. For reason is not the only attribute of man nor is it the only faculty which he habitually employs for the ascertainment of truth. Moral and spiritual faculties are of no less importance in their respective spheres, even of everyday life; faith, trust, and taste are as needful in ascertaining truth as to character and beauty as is reason. Indeed, we may take it that reason is concerned in ascertaining truth only where causation is concerned; the appropriate organs for its ascertainment where anything else is concerned belong to the moral and spiritual region." ...

So also the late Frederic Myers who, through contact with science and her methods, lapsed like so many others from the faith of his birth, and after sounding the perilous deeps of psychology was forced irresistibly back to hold it in far greater fullness than ever before. "I venture now," he says in the epilogue to his last great work, "*on a bold saying; for I predict that in consequence of the new evidence all reasonable men a century hence will believe in the Resurrection of Christ, whereas in default of the new evidence, no reasonable men, a century hence, would have believed it*"; and he proceeds to give his reasons for affirming that the phenomena manifested in the life and death of Christ hitherto supposed to be miraculous and supernatural, were not derived from ethical or emotional sources alone, but were representative instances of the working of natural law upon a plane that human faculties have not hitherto become sensible of; that they must need be representative of great structural facts of the Universe involving laws at least as persistent, as identical from age to age, as our known laws of energy or of motion. The central claims of Christianity are now confirmed, he asserts, as never before; and as to the deep disquiet of our time upon religious matters, he contends that our age's restlessness is the restlessness not of senility but of adolescence; it resembles the approach of puberty rather than of death, and he foresees the universal acceptance of a belief in the facts of Christianity as full and complete as is our universal acceptance of the law of gravitation. Lord Kelvin himself has also recently proclaimed that the necessary deduction the physicist and biologist are bound to make from their researches is that "a creative and directive purpose" governs and underlies the whole material universe. Is there anything more pathetic than the words with which Herbert Spencer closes his Autobiography after feeding for seventy years on the husks of agnosticism?

"Thus religious creeds which in one way or another occupy the sphere which rational interpretation seeks to occupy and fails, and fails the more it seeks, I have come to regard with a sympathy based on community of need, feeling the dissent from them results from inability to accept the solutions offered, joined with the wish that solutions could be found."

It is like a faint echo of the Prodigal's cry, "I will arise and go to my Father!" Modern Science then is contributing to the rehabilitation of faith. It tends to justify, not only natural religion, but also that particular "revelation" of the intimacy between man and his Maker, between the visible and the invisible world, which was made manifest by the life and death of the Founder of Christianity. It is teaching us to hold as positive facts demonstrable by the working of natural law, things which hitherto could only be apprehended by faith. It points out that the material universe is but the gross and tangible side of an invisible but, if rightly apprehended, a no less objective universe from which the former draws its chief significance and which may be better understood and negotiated with by the adequate development of even human faculties. It justifies the anticipation already expressed that a century is coming to the birth that may be associated with the Evangelist who insisted upon the essential importance of spirit as opposed to matter. "God is a Spirit," or as the Hindu scriptures (which in the light of modern knowledge can be read with almost as much interest as our own) have it, "the ether in the heart" of men and things; a Spirit to be apprehended not so much, if at all, by the reason as by that spiritual faculty which is immanent in each of His creatures, which may smolder or can be fanned into a flame at the will of the individual, and which in any case must sooner or later fulfill the law of its being by progressive stages like the grosser matter that temporarily encases it. Psychology is showing that union or harmonious relation with the higher universe around us is our true end, and that inner communion, by prayer or otherwise, with the spirit thereof is a process wherein work is capable of being done and is done, and its energy can be induced, nay, even compelled, to flow in and produce effects in the world of phenomena. In every great religion, including the Christian, the ultimate Deity, whatever attributes may be accorded to Him by its followers, is agreed to be inscrutable to and incomprehensible by finite faculties. The highest possible attempt to conceive Him has been and can only be made through the medium of some great personality invested with the greatness of the Divine and the limitations of humanity. For some a Buddha or a Krishna has constituted that medium and pointed the road from the finite to the infinite; for us, the Incomprehensible has been manifested by Him who proclaimed "No man cometh to the Father save through Me . . . I am the Way"; the demonstrator of the connection between, and the interpreter of, the visible and the invisible sections of the Universe.

The other day I was examining the phenomena of radium under the guidance of a distinguished scientist, who has been actively concerned in investigating the properties of that remarkable substance. In the daylight all that was apparent was a few grains of white powder, but on looking at the radium salts in the dark they shone through the glass tube that held them with a steady, luminous glow. As I watched this spectacle and saw the marvelous production of heat and light without any apparent source of energy, this spontaneous radiation of its particles without any appreciable loss to the bulk, this apparent contradiction of the laws of the conservation of energy and the conservation of matter, my scientific mentor said to me: "You are looking at the most wonderful sight in the world!" Exemplified by the radiation of those sparks of matter was what we are led now to believe is the secret of the material universe. That radium had been exhibiting its properties for untold ages in the pitchblende ore of Bavaria; it was transforming itself before my eyes into another form of invisible matter of absolutely different properties; it would continue so to do for apparently interminable time. It indicated that all matter is reducible ultimately to one element, and that the element is in its last resort the product of the invisible and eternal Energy from which the whole visible universe is derived and of which it is a temporary manifestation. Here was the latest triumph, the most recent message of physical science; and I came away with my thoughts.

Afterwards, I passed into the new Roman Catholic Cathedral at Westminster. Worship was being offered with all the sumptuous ritual of the Roman Church and the aid of majestic music that welled from a great choir concealed in some recess of the vast building, while hung in mid-air above the chancel steps was the great golden crucify that spread its arms over a devout assembly comprising men and women of every grade of society and several nationalities. And as I watched the scene with, I fear, some critical detachment of thought from the sacred service, involuntarily the words came again into my mind, "You are looking at the most wonderful sight in the world." For here was the spiritual counterpart of the physical phenomenon I had previously witnessed; the radioactivity of infinitesimal minds towards the central and master intelligence that abides in and energizes the material creation. Natural science knows nothing of spiritual processes; it really gives a final explanation of nothing whatever. All it can do is to bring a little coherency and constancy into the midst of that which is constantly flowing, to explore a little into the enlarging region of the Unknown. And when its last word has been said, whatever be its dicta or conclusions, there still remains the individual human consciousness which feels itself even in its utter littleness to be the microcosm of the whole universe. Science, or rather Rationalism the daughter of Science, has been bidding us to submerge our individual personalities, to consider ourselves ephemeral atoms of the material cosmos. She has asked us to believe we are born into life and consciousness by a complex process of mechanical development and doomed after an hour or two to annihilation, and to live again only so far as the material part of us is concerned in the particles of other material objects molded out of our dust, and as regards our moral part to live in the morality of our posterity. She has utterly repudiated the personal point of view; and religion she has reproached as being a monumental chapter in the history of human egotism. But she is coming round to the recognition of the irrepressible claims of individuality and is beginning to see that *"so long as we deal with the cosmic and the general, we deal only with the symbols of reality, but as soon as we deal with private and personal phenomena as such, we deal with realities in the completest sense of the term."* In other words, the axis of reality runs solely through the egotistic places, and our greatest, most responsible concern is our private, personal destiny after all. The process of complete reconciliation may be slow and painful. The world having tasted the cup of agnosticism, will have to drink it to the dregs before it rises to a clearer vision of realities. Sir Oliver Lodge has said,

"the next century will indeed be fruitful and will be a terrific touchstone of the peoples. . . . Presently something calm and majestic will emerge and the eyes of the man of that day will look on the world with comprehending eyes and will rejoice in

such a contemplation of a scheme of law and order and beauty as is at present possible only to a few."

Before that day comes many changes must needs be wrought in almost every department of human life and thought. If Rationalism abandons some of her unjustifiable pretensions, dogmatic Theology also will have to do the same. The dogmatic framework with which the simple facts of Christianity have been surrounded must undergo no little modification in order to let the picture stand out in its original freshness. Is there not justification for the jibe of a modern satirist that "we change our Parish Councilors every three years, our Articles of Religion we have not overhauled for three hundred?" An official restatement of the significance of the manifestation of Christ in the light of modern cosmological knowledge is an urgent need, and would immensely help both the Churches and those who cannot accept the current principles of interpretation formulated in times of cosmological misconception. Probably no Ecumenical Conference of the Churches could be got together to effect such a restatement or, if got together, would agree upon one. The new outlook will doubtless come into effect by gradual, silent transformation of thought. There will be changes, too, in the social conditions of the world. The present system of irresponsible wealth tending to make the rich richer and the poor poorer, the inordinate lust for material things, the race for money and the degrading desire for social superiority will all have to be paid for and purged away probably by some terrible upheaval before the light of a revived and purer Christianity can shine out. Roman civilization became submerged by the ignorant but more virile barbarians of Northern Europe.

Let us not be too sure that a similar cataclysm will not overwhelm ours. It has been sometimes suggested that the hosts of the great yellow races from the East may someday take their revenge upon the West for the contumely and imperiousness meted out to them. It is a contingency unlikely for many reasons, and please God there will be no more Dark Ages. What seems a much greater probability is a social revolution on the part of the great labor classes of Europe and America that will utterly transform our modern social system, of which selfishness is one of the main features. Such a revolution would destroy many of our modern methods and ideals, but it would overwhelm also much of our present selfishness and materialism. It would be apparently a setback to the world's progress, but it would be a setback only *pour mieux sauter* **(to make a strategic withdrawal)**. And out of it would emerge a new people educated in and disciplined to a practical Christian altruism which in their mundane affairs would be, as the Founder of Christianity intended His system to be, the counterpart of the larger faith in the spiritual aspect of the universe that they would hold.

Such a people helped by a Bible construed in the light of modern knowledge and by a faith which natural science and their own religious instinct have converted into a practical knowledge of God; inspired by the presence of the living Christ; conscious of their close contact with the invisible and the reserves of power that can be drawn upon from the intelligence that fills it; such a people would seem worthy to hold pride of place in this world of ours. To such a development, in my view, the long process of human education is leading. In the meantime, for ourselves. Each must work out his own life according to the light shining within him or that may be given him with increasing experience. Let him for whom current religious ideals suffice, continue, through the clash and conflict of views, to hold, in the words of Bishop Westcott, "a firm faith in Christianity and a firm faith in criticism," knowing that they must both ultimately terminate in a common center. And for him who by temperament or for other honest and sufficient reason cannot for the present go beyond the agnostic position—what is required of him, but that he do justice and love mercy and walk humbly with the best concept of the Highest that he can fashion for himself? Religious thought, whether it be individual or national or universal, is not exempt any more than other institutions from the laws of evolution and natural selection. The fittest will survive and, by its survival, justify its fitness. The process is always painful and strenuous, and through the strain that process entails, Christianity is now passing. The Churches are passing through the greatest ordeal they have been called on to bear. Clerical authority is being called back to careful knowledge of facts. But the hand that has assailed it is turning into an instrument of blessing.

All the conclusions of natural science and scientific criticism are pointing to a God and to the great purpose of his Christ; but they point also to the necessity of apprehending those truths clearly, and of disengaging them from cobwebs of error, misunderstanding and untenable doctrine about them spun by the speculative or perverse brains of schoolmen and theologians in days gone by. And as they point to the old body of dogmatic teaching which the world is now rejecting, they seem to say, "*Why seek ye the living among the dead? He is not here, He is risen, and will be found in a Religion reconstituted on nobler, broader lines of thought, that will be not so much the contradiction as the fuller realization of the old.*" And Science?

Science in Newton's phrase, has been picking up pebbles on the shore of the boundless ocean of knowledge; nay, recently, and especially in regard to the problem of Consciousness, she has been doing more. Amazed at what the tide has washed up, in her eagerness she has sailed out a little way upon the waters, let down her dragnets and drawn up further treasures from the secret places of the deep; treasures that on inspection are justifying the hopes and confirming the beliefs of anxious watchers from the shore. But when her present inquiries are completed; when she has added to our faith knowledge, and we to our knowledge have added wisdom and power, will humanity even then have completed its education? Will it be content to rest even at that stage, thinking it has exhausted knowledge and solved all problems?

Nay! come up hither to this wave-washed mound, And to the furthest flood-brim look with me. Then reach on with thy thought till that be drowned, Miles and miles distant though thy last thought be. And though thy soul sail leagues and leagues beyond, Still, leagues beyond those leagues, there is more sea!

Forgotten Essays

SCIENCE AND THE OCCULT AT THE BRITISH ASSOCIATION

A PERUSAL of the proceedings of the parliament of British scientists recently held at York makes it of interest to consider the bearing that the progressive results of official science have upon the recondite problems which belong to the domain of the super physical and form the subject of psychical research. The inter-relation of the two spheres of investigation is and must needs be very intimate, and the official findings and even tentative pronouncements of either side entail examination, and, if need be, assimilation by the other. As a tunnel bored from opposite sides, Nature may be probed from different points. Sooner or later a juncture will be effected; a nexus established between the obvious and the obscure. It is a commonplace to observe that, within the last twenty-five years, physical science has revolutionized philosophical ideas in regard to the constitution of Nature. A quarter of a century ago a materialistic gospel seemed to many people to be the inevitable heritage of succeeding generations. In the famous presidential address at Belfast in 1874, Tyndall had proclaimed:

"The confession I feel bound to make before you, is that by an intellectual necessity I prolong the vision backward across the boundary of experimental science and discover in matter itself the promise and potency of every form and quality of life."

By 1898, the wheel had come full circle. The then president, Sir W. Crookes, reversed the terms of Tyndall's conclusion and confessed that closer investigation of physical material constrained him to "see in life the promise and potency of all forms of matter." Matter had come to be, demonstrably, a product, not a cause; a temporary resultant or equilibrium of forces, not a reality or thing-in-itself; it was

- 161 -

force, of some description, made manifest and sensible. In 1904, the hypothesis of the electronic constitution of matter and the new problems of thought it involved tempted Mr. A. J. Balfour to make a philosophical survey of the newly achieved results and to indicate the intellectual position one had been driven to assume in consequence. Scientific results, he said, had shown the utterly illusory nature of our sense faculties which, while true to reality upon the physical plane where they had been evolved to perform utilitarian ends, stood in contradiction and were a positive obstacle to the apprehension of realities beyond the reach of sense.

"In order of logic, sense perceptions supply the premises from which we draw our knowledge of the physical world; but, in order of causation, they themselves are effects due to the constitution of our organs of sense; are themselves the product of evolution."

What we see and hear depends not merely on what there is to be seen and heard, but on our eyes and ears. By their help indeed we have attained to science, but in nowise to a self-sufficing system of beliefs, which must be the product of other faculties in us than the purely sensual. Hence, it has come about that the beliefs of all mankind about the material surroundings in which it dwells are not only imperfect but fundamentally wrong. It may seem singular that down to, say, five years ago, our race has, without exception, lived and died in a world of illusions and that its illusions have not been about things remote or abstract, things transcendental or divine, but about what men see and handle, about those plain "matters of fact" among which commonsense daily moves with its most confident step and most self-satisfied smile; a conclusion which constrains one to the belief that, "as natural science grows, it leans more, not less, upon an idealistic conception of the Universe." The trend of scientific thought, then, as revealed by the foregoing utterances, makes it probable that the emergence of phenomena of a metaphysical and metaphysical nature from the condition of ostracism to which they have hitherto been relegated is but a question of time, and that at no remote date they will take their place in the ranks with other problems recognized as legitimate subjects of scientific examination. It was the inevitable tendency of modem physical science to eliminate from its enquiries, and even from its beliefs, everything beyond the reach of sense. To borrow an expression of the mediaeval alchemists, it sought to "fix the volatile." Stem adhesion to this principle has ended in a result of the converse of what was to be expected; it has "volatilized the fixed." Agnosticism in regard to the super sensual is slowly, but perceptibly, becoming displaced by a condition of open-mindedness in which further knowledge of the physical and the accumulating evidence in regard to the super physical may be trusted to make their own impressions and serve for the construction of a larger and surer philosophy than any the human mind has yet been capable of formulating.

Meanwhile, note may be taken of some recent contributions certain departments of recognized science have just made to the general stock of information from which the larger synthesis will eventually be made. It was not to be expected that at the recent meeting of the British Association at York the presidential address, coming as it did from one who has ever been the arch-foe of experimental transcendentalism, would be especially illuminative to those whose views upon the more recondite side of Nature differ from his. Yet Professor Ray Lankester gave an admirable summary of the progress of science in its various branches during the last twenty-five years, and, speaking under the shadow of York Minster, closed upon a pleasing note in claiming that, "men of science seek in all reverence to discover the Almighty, the Everlasting. They claim sympathy and friendship with those who, like themselves, have turned away from the more material struggles of human life and have set their hearts and minds on the knowledge of the Eternal."

On referring to progress in psychology, his combative spirit could not refrain from hurling a dart at those of his eminent colleagues who have felt it their duty to undertake the investigation of psychical problems. "Whilst some enthusiasts have been eagerly collecting ghost stories and records of human illusion and fancy, the serious experimental investigation of the human mind, and its forerunner the animal mind, has been quietly but steadily proceeding in truly scientific channels. The science is still in an early phase—that of the collection of accurate observation and measurements—awaiting the development of great guiding hypotheses and theories"—a remark equally applicable to metaphysical science. It is improbable, and unnecessary, that the jibe should meet, as some of the London press anticipates, with a reply from those at whom it was cast; one of whom recently announced that he had ceased "to shout to the congenitally deaf." One is tempted to repeat the criticism made upon Southey by a venerable Methodist clergyman after reading that author's Life of Wesley: "Sir, thou hast nothing to draw with; and the well is deep."

Two other papers read before sections of the Association appear to contribute information that is of interest to psychical enquirers. In one, Mr. E. Sidney Hartland, the President of the Anthropological Section, addressed himself to the study of the relations of magic and religion. It is unnecessary here to consider his conclusions or his views as to the means by which the religion of civilized races of today (referred to as "a social secretion") has been evolved, but some of the facts he employs are of interest as showing the correspondence between certain beliefs of races living nearer to Nature than we, and some of the results of modem research into human personality. One of the latter is the demonstration of the aura surrounding the human body, a phenomenon claimed to be visible to clairvoyant sight, but the assumption of which appears to be warranted by various methods of experiment. This aura, when in a static, quiescent state, is comparatively colorless and would seem to be the physical vehicle of the subliminal self; it is the agent by means of which are received or communicated those subtle impressions involving sympathy with or antipathy towards other persons, or become translated into presentiments of impending events; and which operates, generally, as might be expected of an apparatus constructed by Nature for the purpose of human wireless telegraphy. Under the stimulus of volition, strong thought or emotion, it becomes dynamic and energized, and is colored according to the nature of the stimulus and the effects of its intense vibration are communicated to our surroundings and even to great distances. It is the factor which makes possible the phenomena of mesmerism and hypnotism, and its presence is indicated by the response which patients in the somnambulic state are wont to make to touching or pinching at some distance from their physical persons. By a trained and adept wielder of will-power obviously considerable influence of either a beneficent or malignant character might be exercised over his fellows and even upon material objects, and indeed it may be assumed that all "miracles" and feats of genuine magic are performed by the employment of this medium, as well as many of the abnormal physical phenomena that occur in the presence of trance mediums. Mr. Hartland indicates that the knowledge of this latent side of personality is quite familiar to certain primitive races who put it to practical use. With some (*e.g.* the Iroquoian tribes of North America) this fluidic atmosphere surrounding every personality is known as Orenda, a word suspiciously akin to Aura. With others (the Melanesians) it is termed Marta, mind power, again a close resemblance to the Sanskrit *Manas*, and the Latin *Mens*.

"A fine hunter was one whose orenda was fine, superior in quality. When he was successful, he was said to baffle or thwart the orenda of the quarry; when unsuccessful, the same was said to have foiled or outmatched his orenda." Again, the Mana "is what works to affect everything which is beyond the ordinary power of men outside the common process of nature; it is present in the atmosphere of life, attaches itself to persons and to things and is manifested by results which can only be attributed to its operation." It underlay the use of amulets and the practice of Taboo; and one may imagine that the origin of notice boards upon private property bearing the familiar legend, "Trespassers will be prosecuted," was the practice of infecting the prohibitory signposts with the owner's aural fluid so as to produce instant punitive effect upon transgressors. When a Malagasy stuck up in his field a figure or scarecrow to keep off robbers, it was not that they might dread prosecution with all the rigor of the law. What was threatened was sickness, mysteriously induced by the power of the owner of the field, or by the power which he had caused to be conjured into the scarecrow. The transference of sickness from one person to another by means of bringing the garments of the diseased into contact with healthy people is one of the favorite methods of "black magic" adopted by unscrupulous Orientals today; as the transmission of health is, in like manner, practiced among ourselves at the present time, in precisely the method adopted in Apostolic times, when "from his (Paul's) body they brought unto the sick handkerchiefs or aprons, so that their diseases departed from them and the evil spirits went out of them" (Acts xix. 12). Mr. Hartland traces all magic, witchcraft and priest craft to superior ability to put orenda to practical use. By his orenda a man bewitched his enemy (or for a consideration someone else's enemy), caused rain or sunshine, raised and protected the crops, gave success in hunting, divined the cause of sickness and cured it, raised the dead, spelt out the future. All Melanesian religion consisted in the getting of mana for one's self or getting it used for one's benefit. The professional magician was he who had acquired the most powerful orenda. The professional priest was he who by study and practice or by prayer and fasting had acquired the favor of the imaginary personalities believed to influence or control the affairs of men—who had, in a word, possessed himself of their orenda. And hence the division of magic into black and white; "black magic" being the use of occult power for selfish personal ends, "white" for beneficent altruistic purposes.

The scriptural miracles and the healing, exorcising and ordaining powers employed, chiefly by the imposition of hands, by the leaders of the early Christian Church, were clearly due to the conscious utility to transmit beneficent power by application of the human aura or personal electric fluid (*the Od of Reichenbach, du Prel and de Rochas*), an appropriate mental condition of receptivity or "faith" being an essential on the part of those who solicited its remedial properties. Of the eternal memory of Nature and the perpetuation in an inanimate matter of its past associations, we have much evidence today through the practice of psychometry. The veneration of relics is based upon sound scientific fact, with which Mr. Hartland shows that the most primitive races are quite conversant. Detached portions of the person, as locks of hair, parings of the fingernails and so forth, were not dead inert matter. They were still endued with the life of the original owner. Nay, garments once worn or other objects which had been in intimate contact with a human being were penetrated by his personality and remained, as it were, with him for good or ill. Mr. Hartland's paper might appropriately have been read to an audience of psychical researchers. Its significant feature is the evidence of the existence in man, however primitive, of subtle potencies and attributes of which civilized races have lost the sight but not the use. Those potencies and attributes must needs be, in their physical essence, of an electric or magnetic nature. How are we to explain their existence? From the fact that living organisms are continuous generators of electricity, the radiations of which necessarily impinge upon and convey impressions to other organisms.

Walter L. Wilmshurst

This seems to be the conclusion to be drawn from the important paper read before the Physiological Section of the Association by Professor Gotch, whose main purpose, however, was quite alien to furnishing explanations of occult phenomena. His paper was a powerful criticism of the views of those who assume that living organisms are actuated by an indwelling directive vital force existing independently of the forces automatically generated by chemical and physical processes in the organism. The professor's views savor of Haeckelianism and are obviously directed against those expounded in Sir O. Lodge's recent work Life and Matter, which place life in a separate category from matter and regard it as a controlling and directive force as opposed to a mere product of automatic processes. The hypothesis of "vitalism"—the assumption of "animal spirits" or anything amounting to a soul as an entity distinguishable from the body—has been the bugbear of most scientists for some time past. The heresy was thought to have been scotched, but latterly, the Professor complains, a school of "neo-vitalists" has arisen which cannot reconcile "events of a peculiarly mystic character" and certain "transcendental phenomena" with the dogma of orthodox physiology, and who have most unjustifiably "fabricated for them, out of their own conceit, a special and exclusive realm."

There is no more justification, the Professor urges, for branding as hopeless all further physical and chemical investigation of these phenomena, by attributing them to vital directive forces, than there was formerly for the opponents of evolution, who discredited that hypothesis in favor of that of special creations, because of gaps and imperfections in the paleontological record which more recent research has filled up. The Professor's conclusion is that the sum of the phenomena constituting life arises from "a purely physico-chemical process of an electrolytic character," and that the difference between "life" and "not life" was not due to the presence in the former of a new form of energy,

but to the circumstance that a mode of energy, displayed in the nonliving world, occurred in colloidal electrolytic structures of great chemical complexity. There was a natural prejudice against the adoption of this view, but such prejudice should surely be mitigated by the consideration that their full admission of physiology into the realm of natural science, by forcing a more comprehensive recognition of the harmony of Nature, was invested with intellectual grandeur. If objective phenomena formed the subject matter of the physiologist, then the "legitimate materialism of science" must constitute his working hypothesis, and his well-defined purpose must be to adapt and apply the methods of physics and chemistry for the analysis of such phenomena as he could detect in all physiological tissues, including the nervous system. The trend of such a strictly physiological analysis was towards a conception in which the highest animal appeared as an automaton composed of differentiated structures exquisitely sensitive to the play of physical and chemical surroundings.

Whether future physiological research will confirm this conclusion and adequately explain, not alone mystical and transcendental phenomena, but the deep problems of consciousness and will, factors which now preclude many thinkers from accepting the Professor's view, time alone will show. His address assuredly makes out a strong case for the contention that "nervous processes do not in their essence differ from processes occurring elsewhere in both the living and non-living worlds," a contention that may well be true, but that is apt to lead to materialism those who do not perceive that physiology and biology can at most present but a partial explanation of life, and that the testimony of other branches of science must be heard before a final estimate is made. Meanwhile, even though the evidence of any given branch is apparently adverse to idealistic conceptions—for the hearts of humanity will not be satisfied merely with spectacles of "intellectual grandeur" offered by an impersonal, automatic universe—it is possible to note the trend the analytical examination of objective Nature is taking.

Physics demonstrates that so much of it as is inert is but the temporary and sensible expression of a force which, for the present, we are content vaguely to describe by the term electricity. The various sciences treating of organisms and the phenomena they exhibit point to precisely the same conclusion; their corporeality is electrically constituted, and their actions, whether elementary and utilitarian, or mystical and transcendental, are, physically considered, due to motion of an electrical character. Both the inert and the organic are modifications of one and the same force, but in the organism that force is endowed with consciousness, and in the case of man, with personality. Now force, whether personalized or depersonalized, is, we know, an expression of will, and will, in turn, is unimaginable except as an attribute of personality. Unification, then, of the material and the immaterial, of the manifest and sensible, and of the occult and elusive, in a Personality in which all things must needs live and move and have their being, is the goal to which all science is, unconsciously and by various paths, progressing. Backward eddies, appearing here and there upon the surface of the stream, only serve to mark the intensity of the general forward-moving current, and indeed are a part of it. Men of science specializing in certain work and blinded to other phases and phenomena of Nature than those they are immediately concerned with, none the less advance the tide of knowledge. They check indulgence in extravagant and premature assumptions, and often the very antagonism displayed by some of the distinguished scientists to occult and psychical problems indicates that the latter are "knocking at the door" and clamoring for consideration. By the time the British Association next meets under the shadow of York Minster it is not improbable that they will have gained admission. A significant hint was thrown out to its members by the Bishop of Ripon, who, as one equally conversant with official science and the adumbrations of truth disclosed by psychical research, could effectively quote Huxley's caution, that "in contemplating the all-enveloping mystery of life we know little of the forms of existence and that perhaps in time we shall be flung into contact with forms of life of which we now can have no possible conception, and know no more about than the worm in the flower-pot on a London balcony knows of the life of the great city around it."

FINIS

Walter L. Wilmshurst

Author and Managing Editor

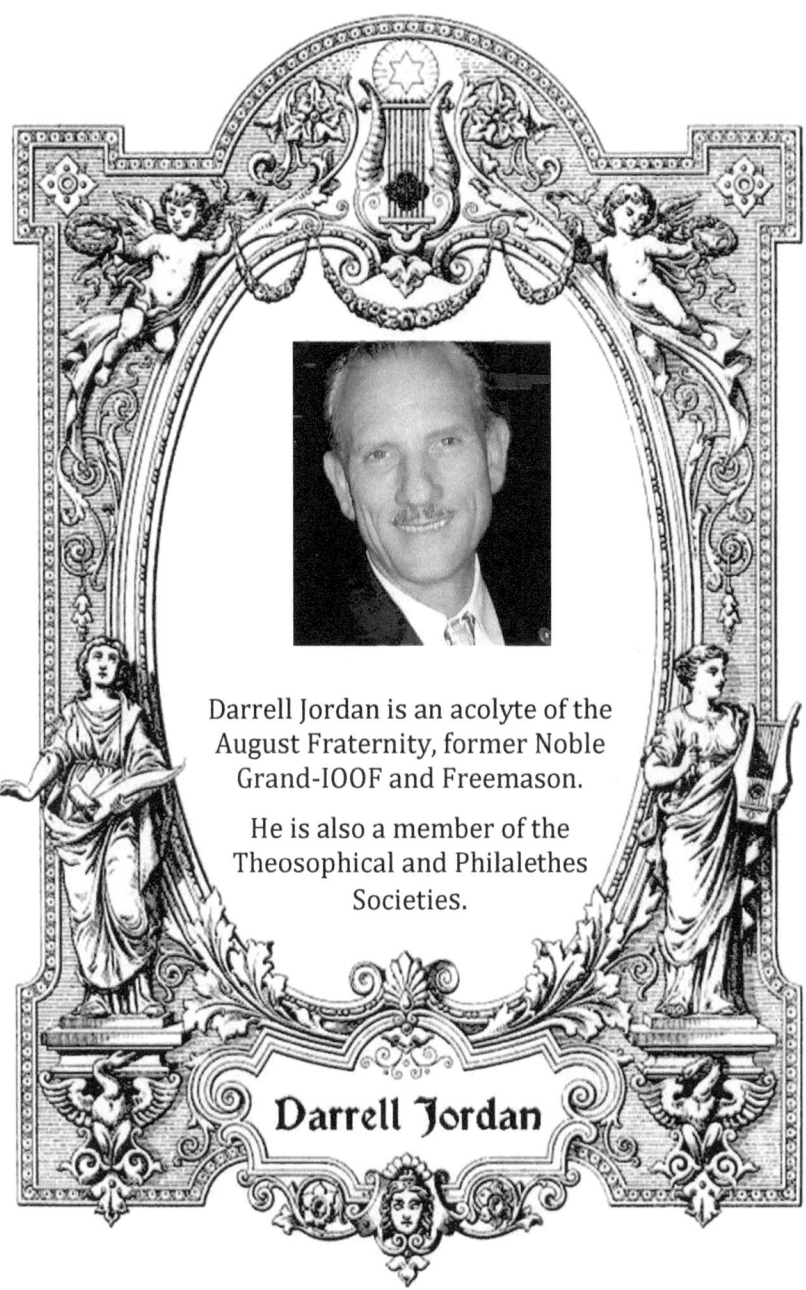

Darrell Jordan is an acolyte of the August Fraternity, former Noble Grand-IOOF and Freemason.

He is also a member of the Theosophical and Philalethes Societies.

Manly P. Hall All-Seeing Eye Series

Manly P. Hall Seeker of More Intelligent Life Series

Books by the Managing Editor

Hiram E. Buttler
Exoteric Christianity

Arthur Waite
Forgotten Essays

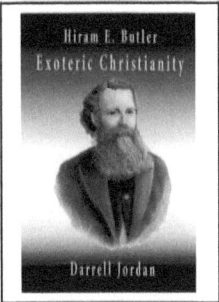
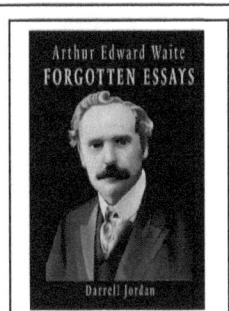

The Initiates Speak

George Oliver
Masonic Writings

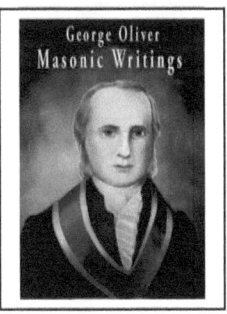

For the latest books, visit:
Parallel47North.com/collections/esoteric-books

Contact: Info@Parallel47North.com

Hiram E. Buttler

Arthur Waite

The Initiates Speak
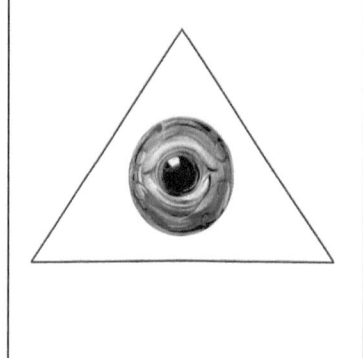

George Oliver

Forgotten Essays

Portraits and Illustrations by the Artist

Manly P. Hall

Artist Portfolio:
JessicaNaomiDesigns.com